D1141105

Bestall

This book belongs to

....

CONTENTS

Edited by Stephanie Milton. Designed by Martin Aggett.
Cover illustrated by Stuart Trotter.
Endpapers illustrated by Alfred Bestall.

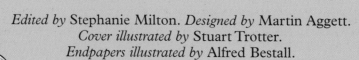

THE 80th RUPERT ANNUAL

EXPRESS NEWSPAPERS

EGMONT

We bring stories to life

Published in Great Britain 2015 by Egmont UK Limited
The Yellow Building, 1 Nicholas Road, London W11 4AN
Rupert Bear™ & © 2015 Classic Media Distribution Limited/Express Newspapers.
All Rights Reserved.

ISBN 978 1 4052 7900 0
60317/1
Printed in Italy

All rights reserved. No part of this publication may be reproduced, stored in a retrieval system or transmitted, in any form or by any means, mechanical, photocopying, recording or otherwise, without the prior permission of the publisher and copyright holder. Stay safe online. Any website addresses listed in this book are correct at the time of going to print. However, Egmont is not responsible for content hosted by third parties. Please be aware that online content can be subject to change and websites can contain content that is unsuitable for children. We advise that all children are supervised when using the internet.

No. 80

RUPERT and

*"Oh, do please, Mummy, say I may
Go to the Wise Old Goat's today."*

The Wise Old Goat has a nephew, Billy, and one morning Billy turns up at the Bears' house to ask if Rupert would like to join him in a hike to his uncle's castle in the hills. "I haven't seen him for ages," he says. "We can stay the night." "Oh, Mummy, may I?" Rupert begs. "Well, if you're sure Billy's uncle won't mind . . . " she says. And so later that day after a long walk, from Nutwood, the chums reach the Wise Old Goat's castle.

the Mulp Gulper

So off they tramp across the fells
To where young Billy's uncle dwells.

"Hey, Uncle, I've brought Rupert Bear!"
But there's no one to answer there.

Billy hurries ahead to tell his uncle that he has brought Rupert. But there is no answer to his ring at the bell and only silence when he goes in and calls. "Maybe he's busy in his workshop," Rupert suggests. But when they search the house there is no sign of the Wise Old Goat. So they wait but still he doesn't come and at last they decide to go to bed. "He usually leaves a note if he's away for any time," Billy muses.

They wait but no one comes and so
The pals decide to bed they'll go.

RUPERT IS CHASED BY A BIRD

*When still he's not come back next day
The pals decide they must not stay.*

*They've hardly set off down the track
Before a great bird turns them back.*

*The two turn tail and fairly scorch
Back to the shelter of the porch.*

*Then back and forth the great bird flies.
"It's 'saying' something!" Rupert cries.*

Rupert and Billy hoped when they fell asleep that the Wise Old Goat might be back when they wakened. But no. And now they are really worried. "I don't like this," Rupert says. "I vote we go straight back to Nutwood for help." So as soon as they have had a bite to eat the two pals set out for home.

They haven't gone far, though, when a shadow falls over them. A great bird is just overhead. And as they try to walk on it swoops angrily.

"Run for it!" shouts Rupert. But their attempt to dash down the path back to Nutwood only makes the great bird swoop lower and squawk more angrily. So they turn and dash for the shelter of the castle doorway. Then the bird does something very strange. While the pals look on from the safety of the rocks near the door, it flies towards the mountains, returns and repeats the performance several times. "I don't think it was attacking us," Rupert says. "It's been trying to tell us something!"

RUPERT FOLLOWS THE BIRD

Then on the sill it comes to sit.
It wants the chums to follow it.

They send a note, their folk to tell.
What's going on and that they're well.

The bird returns and they set out
Still wondering what it's all about.

"This stream supplies our river, though
I must say, it seems rather low."

Rupert and Billy wave at the bird to show that they understand it wants to tell them something. Then they go back into the house where the bird appears and settles on a window sill. "Wait! I know you!" exclaims Billy. "You're my uncle's messenger bird!" The bird nods. "And you want us to go with you, right?" Rupert asks. Again a nod. That does it. In a moment Rupert is giving the bird a note to take to their parents to say what's happening, while Billy makes sandwiches.

It doesn't take the bird long to get back from Nutwood and Billy and Rupert are waiting, their knapsacks packed with food for the journey ahead.

At once the bird turns towards the mountains and the chums follow. Higher and higher it leads them until they reach a stream. "I know this," says Billy. "It's the stream that feeds our own Nutwood River. But I'm sure it was bigger last time I saw it." Now the bird turns upstream. It seems anxious to press on.

RUPERT FINDS THE SPRING DRY

It seems the spring is running dry.
This level should be much more high.

At last the bird stops where the spring
Just wets the rocks, a feeble thing.

It wants them to go in the cave.
Now neither of them feels so brave.

The bird makes such a fuss that though
They're frightened they just have to go.

The bird leads them higher into the mountains to a little lake which Billy calls a tarn. "It feeds the stream we've been following," he explains. "But it's very low." "Where does its water come from?" Rupert asks. "From a spring that starts higher up," Billy tells him. And rhat, it turns out, is where the spring is a mere trickle and when at last they reach the cave where it starts there is hardly any water at all.

But the bird does not fly on. It perches on a rock outside the cave. "Well, what now?" Rupert asks. For answer the bird flaps its great wings and flies into the cave. The pals look at each other. And their looks say that they don't much fancy the idea of following it. But the bird won't have that. When it finds that it isn't being followed it emerges from the cave with a great squawk and sweeps into the gloom once more. "I—I suppose we'd better go in," quavers Rupert.

RUPERT'S OLD FRIEND IS FOUND

It hovers near a pile of rocks.
It flaps its wings and how it squawks!

They wonder what they're going to find,
Approach the rocks and peer behind.

The Wise Old Goat! He stirs. He moans.
"Oh, dear! My poor old head!" he groans.

While checking on the spring he fell.
The bird was with him – just as well!

Inside the cave Rupert and Billy wait for their eyes to get used to the gloom. When they can see they are not much happier. The cave seems to go deep into the mountain. They can see traces of the spring which has stopped running now. Then they jump as the messenger bird which is hovering above a boulder squawks loudly. "It's showing us something," Rupert whispers. Very cautiously he leads the way to the boulder and peers behind it. "Look at this!" he gasps.

Lying behind the boulder is the Wise Old Goat! "Oh, Uncle, what's happened?" Billy cries. At the sound of Billy's voice his uncle stirs. "Oh, my head!" he moans. The pals help him to sit up and Rupert produces his water bottle. The Wise Old Goat drinks from it. "That's better," he sighs. Then he tells the pals how he came up to see why the stream was drying up, saw that the spring had stopped, entered the cave, slipped on a rock and banged his head. Luckily the bird was with him.

RUPERT HAS A PLAN

*Before he fell he saw something
Had been done to divert the spring.*

*They go to look, and, sure enough,
They find that someone's built a trough.*

*"Let's turn it back and maybe then
They'll come to change it round again."*

*They settle down their watch to keep.
But no one comes. They fall asleep.*

Seeing its master safe the bird flies off again leaving him with the pals. "Just before I fell," says the Wise Old Goat, "I spied something strange. The spring had not actually dried up – look!" He points into the cave where the chums can just make out a sort of structure. They go closer to find the spring gushing freely into a wooden trough which disappears into the cave. Rupert gasps: "Someone has changed the way it goes!" "But who?" Billy whispers nervously.

"Whoever it was went to a lot of trouble to do it," says Billy's uncle. "But why?" Then Rupert has one of his ideas. "If they want it so much they'd be bound to come and see what's wrong if we change the direction of the stream back again." "Good idea," agrees the Wise Old Goat, and within a few minutes the chums have turned part of the trough so that the spring once more flows out of the cave. Then by the light of the Goat's pocket lantern they settle to wait.

He starts awake but not before
The spring has been turned round once more!

When they get up to look they find
Someone has left a note behind.

"We need the water," says the note.
"And we do!" says the Wise Old Goat.

Again they turn the water round,
But leave a message to be found.

Well, the three friends wait and wait and try hard to stay awake. But nothing happens and, of course, they fall asleep.

Suddenly Rupert is awake. What was that? Like scurrying feet disappearing into the depths of the cave? By the dim light of the lantern he looks around. Next moment the others start up at his cry – "The spring! It's been switched back again!" When the friends scramble to their feet and go to look, Rupert spots something on a rock.

"Look! A note!" he cries. "It says, 'Please do not take back your water. We need it very badly'." "They seem friendly," says Billy. But his uncle looks solemn. "We must have the water, too," he says. "Without it the river in Nutwood would dry up. We must switch it back." But while the chums are yet again changing the direction of the spring, he writes a reply on the back of the note: "Sorry, we must have spring too, but we want to help you. Tell us how."

RUPERT MEETS THE SPELIES

The plan is they'll pretend to sleep.
In fact, a careful watch they'll keep.

They doze off and when they come round
They find they're pinioned to the ground.

"We've found your note and now we see
You're friendly so we'll set you free."

From far away there comes a roar.
They rush to turn the spring once more.

Now the Wise Old Goat explains his plan to the chums. He will leave his note where it will be found when they mysterious strangers come back to find out why the spring has been switched once again. "We shall pretend to be asleep." But although the three lie very still, just now and then opening an eye to see what is happening, nothing stirs and they fall asleep.

They waken to a shock. They are tied to the ground by strong cords. And someone's coming!

Fearfully the friends listen to the approaching footsteps. But although the figures who appear from the depths of the cave are among the oddest Rupert has seen, they look friendly. Their leader addresses Rupert: "Sorry we tied you up. We didn't know what you might do . . . but now we've seen your note." Meanwhile his companions are untying the three friends. Suddenly – an angry roar from deep in the cave. Immediately the little creatures rush towards the spring.

RUPERT HEARS AN AWFUL NOISE

Until the trough's been turned around
The rocks with angry roars resound.

"Mulp Gulper is a creature who'll
Burn down our homes if not kept cool."

The Wise Old Goat says, "If we may,
Let's see this creature. Lead the way!"

"We're Spelies . . . " starts the little guide.
A strange noise halts them in full stride.

Looking terrified, the little creatures heave round the trough under the spring so that once more the water runs into the cave. Soon the roaring sinks to a rumble, then silence. The one who seems to be the leader apologises: "I really am sorry. I knew this would happen if we couldn't have the spring water . . . " "But what made that noise?" asks the Wise Old Goat. "The Mulp Gulper," comes the reply. "If the mulps aren't kept cool it may burn down our homes! If it weren't for the wretched creature we shouldn't need the spring water." The Wise Old Goat nods. "If we're to help you I think we should see this Mulp Gulper," he says. "Very well," says the other and, switching on the lamp on his head, turns back into the cave. "We are the Spelies," he explains as they go. "The caves are our homes. Well, some time ago the Mulp Gulper came . . . " Just then the friends hear a greedy, slurping, guzzling sound from somewhere not far ahead of them.

RUPERT SEES THE MULP GULPER

Then forward to the edge they creep,
And down into a cavern peep.

And there's Mulp Gulper, great fat brute!
Devouring piles of soaking fruit.

They're wrong-way plums the dragon gulps,
And known, the Spelie says, as mulps.

"If not kept cool that beast breathes fire.
What happens – look! – is really dire!"

The sound grows as the cave gets wider and lighter. Ahead, Rupert and the others can make out a big, well-lit cavern with the doors of little homes let into its walls. The Spelie stops them, steals forward and peers over into the cavern. Then he beckons to the friends. "There," he points, "is the Mulp Gulper, gulping mulps as fast as we can pick them." And there below is a fat dragon with, before it, a great pile of fruit being soaked by spring water from the trough.

"Are those plums?" whispers Rupert. "Sort of," says the Spelie. "But they grow the wrong way round – down into the earth." Below, Spelies are dumping barrowloads of the fruit in front of the dragon. "It dotes on them and we can't get rid of it," says the Spelie. "What's worse is that it's a fire-breathing dragon and the mulps have to be soaked to keep its insides cool or it breathes fire . . ." He points to a scorched doorway.

"I've an idea," says the Wise Old Goat.

RUPERT TASTES A MULP

Each tries a mulp. The test is brief!
The taste is foul beyond belief!

The Wise Old Goat says, "Now, you two,
I have a little job for you."

"Go to my workshop, that's your task,
And bring back here a special flask."

The stream before was hardly high.
But now, they see, it's almost dry.

The Wise Old Goat whispers to the Spelie leader who, a moment later, hands a mulp to each of the three friends. "Try them," says the Wise Old Goat and nods to the chums. All three bite into the fruit and . . . "Ugh!" they chorus, spitting out what they've bitten off. "I've never tasted anything so awful!" gasps Rupert as he and Billy wash away the taste with mouthfuls of spring water. The Wise Old Goat meanwhile is smiling and writing busily in his notebook.

When the Wise Old Goat has finished writing he says to Rupert and Billy, "I want you to fetch something from my workshop. This will tell you how to find it." He hands Rupert a page from his notebook. A few minutes later the friends are on their way out of the cave. On their way to the Wise Old Goat's home they pass the tarn. By now it is almost empty. "We must hurry if Nutwood river isn't to dry up altogether," says Rupert. On they go by the stream, now a mere trickle.

17

RUPERT IS SENT ON AN ERRAND

At last they reach the castle where
They hurry to the workshop there.

"Yes, it's the right one, I can tell.
I say, what's that delightful smell?"

The Wise Old Goat is waiting when
The two pals reach the cave again.

Fixed to a branch beside the trough
He's rigged a bag of porous stuff.

Rupert and Billy make straight for the workshop when they reach the Wise Old Goat's home. Rupert studies the note he has been given. "The cupboard in the corner," he reads. "That's it," he points. When the pals open it there is such a lovely smell. They sniff happily. "Now the round flask from the top shelf," Rupert reads. "Yes, here it is." He lifts it down carefully. "Now let's get some bread and cheese and hurry back to the cave," he tells Billy.

And so Rupert and Billy start the long haul back to the cave, carrying the flask between them. "What do you think it is?" Billy asks. "I can't imagine," Rupert says. "But everything in that cupboard had the loveliest smell."

The Wise Old Goat is waiting for them and leads them into the cave. He has been busy while they've been gone. He has fixed a branch to the trough and from it hung a fine mesh bag. "Good, you've brought the right stuff," he says.

*They see the contents emptied out
And wonder what it's all about.*

*The drops ooze through, a moment cling,
Then drop into the rushing spring.*

*And now, they're told, they wait, but not
How long they must, nor yet for what.*

*Then suddenly that awful roar,
But much worse than it was before.*

The chums still have no idea of how the Wise Old Goat means to get rid of the Mulp Gulper and he is not offering any clues. Smiling, he takes the flask and opens it. The smell is quite delicious. Then he empties the contents into the mesh bag over the trough. For a while nothing happens then slowly globules of thick golden liquid drip from the bag into the swiftly-flowing water. Rupert watches, fascinated. The smell is one of the nicest he has ever come across.

"Now," says the Wise Old Goat, "we sit and wait." "Wait for what?" Rupert asks as the others settle themselves on the rocks. But Billy's uncle only smiles his gentle, mysterious smile.

Then when Rupert thinks he can't stand not knowing for another moment, there comes a great, echoing roar of rage from the cavern where the Mulp Gulper is. Everyone jumps – except the Wise Old Goat. "Ah, that is exactly what I hoped for," he says with a smile.

RUPERT SEES THE GULPER FLEE

There is – as to the noise they race –
A smile upon the Wise Goat's face.

The mulps it so enjoyed before
It spits out with disgusted roar.

It grabs its tum. It's plain to tell
Mulp Gulper does feel most unwell.

"It won't eat mulps again. Don't fear,
You'll never see that brute back here!"

"Oh dear, something's upset the wretched beast!" says the Spelies' leader. "We must see what's happened!" And he leads the rush back to the cavern. Rupert, Billy and the Wise Old Goat hurry after them. The two pals are alarmed. But not Billy's uncle.

When at last they look down into the cavern they can hardly believe their eyes. The dragon is still gulping great mouthfuls of mulps, but as fast as it does it spits them out again with a roar of disgust.

"The water's still running on the mulps, so that can't have upset it," Rupert says. "But that is exactly what has upset it," counters the Wise Old Goat. And before he can say anything more, the Mulp Gulper, looking extremely unhappy, clutches its fat tummy, gives a long, low moan and dashes out of the cavern. The Spelies burst into cheers and the Wise Old Goat says, "I'm quite sure it will never fancy mulps again and that you will never see it back here."

RUPERT TASTES THE MIXTURE

The Wise Old Goat's the hero now!
Just hear the Spelies' happy row!

"That stuff," says Rupert, "must taste grim!"
"Then try it," his friend urges him.

"Well, though it made the Gulper sick,
I can at least try one small lick."

He dips it. Licks it. But – what's this?
The taste is lovely – super – bliss!

The Spelies surround the Wise Old Goat, cheering and wishing they were big enough to pat him on the back. But he shakes his head and says, "No time to waste. We must turn the spring or the Nutwood river will dry up." As the Spelies rush to do this Rupert points to the bag over the trough. "That's the stuff that got rid of the Mulp Gulper, isn't it?" The Wise Old Goat nods. "Then we'd better not have it in our water," says Rupert. "Why not?" smiles his old friend.

"Why not?" repeats Rupert. "I should have said that was plain. The Mulp Gulper was enjoying his mulps until that stuff got on them. Then look what happened to him." "Come here," says the Wise Old Goat. "Now dip your finger into the bag and taste it." Very cautiously Rupert does as he's asked. The stuff in the bag feels a bit like honey when you stick your finger in it (which you shouldn't). Even more cautiously Rupert licks his finger. "Oooh! Lovely!" he breathes.

21

"Because it loved the mulps, I knew
The Gulper would detest this brew."

The Spelies shout as our three go,
"When you need help just let us know!"

And now the spring is flowing free,
That's more like how the tarn should be.

"Most odd. The river fell and then
Quite suddenly filled up again!"

Now the Wise Old Goat explains: "The stuff we put in the water is my invention – a mixture of the loveliest tastes you can imagine. I saw that any creature that liked the mulp's awful taste would find this mixture sickening and hateful. I was right!"

Later when the three friends set off for home the Spelies come out of their cave to cheer them on their way. "Any time we can help you let us know and we'll do it!" their leader calls.

When Rupert and the others reach the tarn the little mountain lake is beginning to fill nicely, and the stream from it is running swiftly again down to Nutwood and its river.

At supper time that night Mr Bear tells Rupert: "Strange thing happened today. The water in the river dropped badly. We were frightened it would dry up altogether. Suddenly it has started to fill again. Odd, isn't it?" "Just wait 'til they hear the full story," Rupert thinks. The End.

RUPERT
and the
Coral Crown

RUPERT SPIES A SEA SERPENT

One morning, Rupert wakes to find
A fierce storm rages on outside.

The Bears hear tell that there may be
A serpent swimming in the sea.

Then Rupert points excitedly.
"The Serpent's right there! Can you see?"

"This rock pool here is where I'll stay,
In case it comes into the bay."

The Bears are enjoying their annual summer holiday at the seaside until, one morning, they wake to find a fierce storm is raging outside. "This is very odd weather for August," Rupert thinks as he dresses. Rupert and Mr Bear head out to the beach, which is covered in debris from the storm. As they wander through the crowds they hear rumours that a serpent has been spotted among the waves. The little bear peers through a telescope on the seafront, hoping to catch a glimpse.

A moment later, Rupert spots a large shape swimming near the shore, and it is a shape he recognises. "Daddy, look!" he says, pointing excitedly. "My old friend, the Sea Serpent, is right there! Can you see?" They move down the beach to get a better view. "So he is!" Mr Bear replies. But a moment later the Serpent disappears from view. "Is it all right if I stay here by this rock pool, in case he comes back?" asks Rupert. "Yes," agrees Mr Bear. "I'll be back up on the beach."

RUPERT MEETS A SPRITE

While Rupert's rock pooling, he hears
A noise, and then a sprite appears.

"Hi, what's that? Do you need some help?"
Says Rupert. The sprite gives a yelp.

Poor Rupert gasps. To his dismay,
It seems he's scared the sprite away.

On closer look, it's plain to see
The object's old – a heavy key.

Rupert is absorbed in his rock pooling, hoping to see some crabs or a starfish, when he hears the sound of someone struggling nearby. He turns around and, to his surprise, spots a tiny creature on a nearby rock. It looks like a sea sprite who is trying to pull an object that is stuck in one of the rocks. Rupert carefully makes his way towards it. "Hi!" he calls as he approaches the sprite. "What have you found there? Do you need some help to pull it free?"

But Rupert's friendly greeting startles the sprite. With a yelp, it dashes off and jumps into the sea. "I didn't mean to scare you!" Rupert calls after it, but it keeps its distance and won't come back to the rock. He peers at the object it was trying to lift – it is an old, heavy-looking key. "Whatever can this be doing here?" he wonders aloud. With some effort, he manages to pull the key out of the rock. It looks like it has been there for quite some time.

RUPERT FINDS AN OLD KEY

The moment Rupert pulls it free,
The Serpent rises from the sea!

"The storm's unearthed a shipwreck, and
We need you to give us a hand."

"This key I found lodged in the rock,
I think it might just fit the lock!"

They set off back to Nutwood, where
The pair explain to Mrs Bear.

As Rupert is pulling the key free, the Serpent leaps out of the sea behind him. "Gosh!" Rupert splutters by way of greeting. "You gave me a fright!" "Rupert, the storm has unearthed a pirate ship, wrecked on the sea bed!" the Serpent tells him. "We've seen a large treasure chest inside, which might contain the crown that was stolen from the Sea King by the pirates!" "How exciting!" says Rupert. "Yes. But we need your help to open the chest," the Serpent says.

Rupert gasps. "But this key looks like it would fit an old chest! Well, we will need to dive down to the wreck, and I think my friend Sailor Sam will be able to help us there. I'll pay him a visit, then come straight back." The Serpent nods, so Rupert dashes back to Mr Bear and tells him everything, then they set off back to Nutwood where they explain to Mrs Bear. She takes a closer look at the key. "It certainly looks old," she agrees. "I expect you're right. Sam will be able to help."

RUPERT VISITS SAILOR SAM

Across the common Rupert runs,
Then stops to greet one of his chums.

Now Rupert dashes on to see
His friend Sam, and show him the key.

Intrigued, Sam takes a closer look
Then reaches for a heavy book.

"I have a hunch, but let me check
In my old book of pirate wrecks."

Rupert dashes off towards Sam's house, across Nutwood Common. On the way he runs into one of his chums, Bill Badger. "Where are you off to in such a hurry?" Bill enquires. "To see Sailor Sam!" Rupert replies, showing Bill the key and telling him about the pirate wreck. Bill is very excited and Rupert promises to let him know what happens, then says a hasty goodbye. When he gets to Sam's house he tells him everything and asks if he might be able to help him dive down to the wreck.

"Well, this is exciting!" Sam exclaims. "Let me take a closer look at that key." Rupert hands it to him and Sam studies it carefully. "Yes, it's very possible this belongs to the chest," he tells Rupert. "It's the right size and design. Come inside, while I dig out my old book of pirate shipwrecks. I have a hunch I know which wreck it is that has been uncovered." So the pair head inside and Sam digs out a very old, very large book to check if his suspicions are correct.

RUPERT AND SAM VISIT CAPTAIN WALRUS

Says Sam, "Just as I thought – it's clear,
The spot you mentioned is right here!"

"This diving suit's too small for me,
But you would fit in easily!"

They load Sam's car without delay,
And set off back to Sandy Bay.

The pair will need help with the plan.
And Captain Walrus is their man!

Sam also gets out some nautical charts to cross-reference the position of the shipwreck, and the pair sit down to study them. Sam is soon convinced that the spot Rupert mentioned is the site of a very old pirate wreck, and the chest could well contain some very valuable treasure indeed. He dashes out of the room and returns a moment later, carrying an old diving suit. "This is far too small for me now, but you would fit in easily!" he tells Rupert. "Splendid!" says Rupert, excitedly.

They load the books, maps and the diving suit into Sam's car, then Sam drives them back down to Sandy Bay. They soon track down Captain Walrus and tell him about the treasure chest and show him the key. "We need your help to sail out to the spot and dive down to the chest. Might you be able to take us out on your glass-bottomed boat?" Sam asks. "Of course!" Captain Walrus agrees immediately. "It's been a good while since I used my boat for such an exciting expedition!"

RUPERT GOES OUT ON A BOAT

The three friends set sail on their quest
To find the shipwreck and the chest.

"The Serpent must be here somewhere,"
Says Rupert. "Yes! Look! Over there!"

It disappears from view, and then
Appears under the boat again.

The Serpent grins, as if to say,
"Just follow me, I'll lead the way!"

Captain Walrus hurries off to ready the boat, then invites Rupert and Sam on board. He proudly shows them the glass bottom and the clear view it gives of the sea directly below. Then the three friends set sail from Sandy Bay. As they head out to sea they keep their eyes peeled for a glimpse of the Serpent. "He must be here somewhere," Rupert mutters. Then he sees a shape between the waves. "Over there!" he cries, as the Serpent surfaces for a moment.

But as soon as they have spotted the Serpent it disappears again. There is no sign of it above the water, so they crouch down to look through the glass bottom of the boat. They see nothing for a few moments, but then Sam spots a large, moving shape. "Down there!" he cries. "I think I see him!" A shape is moving towards the glass, and a moment later the Serpent's grinning face comes into view. He nods his head down towards the sea bed, inviting Rupert to follow him.

RUPERT DIVES INTO THE SEA

And Sam asks Rupert, "Are you sure?"
"Oh, yes, the suit looks quite secure."

"This hoist here will do perfectly,
To lower you into the sea."

They peer below the boat once more.
Say Rupert, "Here's the spot, I'm sure."

So Rupert jumps into the sea.
The Serpent greets him happily.

"Are you sure you want to go down by yourself, Rupert?" Sam asks. "Oh, yes, I've no doubt your diving suit is quite secure," Rupert smiles, so Sam and Captain Walrus help him into it. "I have a hoist that we can use to lower you into the sea," the Captain tells Rupert. "Yes, this will do nicely if we tie a length of rope around your middle," Sam agrees. "It'll be quite safe, I do know how to tie a good knot." Sam carefully loops the rope around the little bear.

As Sam makes sure the rope is secure, Rupert peers down into the sea to check that the Serpent hasn't disappeared. He is still there, circling just below them. Rupert puts on his diving helmet and checks his air supply is working. "We're all ship-shape and ready to go!" Captain Walrus smiles. Rupert gives a nod, and the two men begin to lower him carefully over the side of the boat. Once in the sea, the Serpent greets him happily. "Follow me, I'll lead the way!" the Serpent says.

RUPERT FINDS THE CHEST

As they descend, to their surprise,
They spot a face they recognise.

It's Rupert's friend the Merboy, and
He's come along to lend a hand.

The Merboy says, "Just follow me!
The chest is here! Now try the key!"

He tries the key, it gives a click,
And three turns clockwise do the trick.

The pair swim downwards and soon the shipwreck comes into sight. As they reach the ship's deck, another old friend appears. "Hello, Rupert!" the Merboy calls. "I heard you were looking for the chest – I can lead you there!" He unties Rupert from the rope so that he is free to swim inside the wreck, then leads the way off deck and down to the side of the ship. There is a large hole in the side of the ship, and several pieces of timber have come loose.

In amongst the loose timber is a large, old, wooden chest with a rusty lock. It has clearly been on the bottom of the ocean for a long time and they swim towards it excitedly. "This is it," the Merboy says. "Try the key!" So Rupert tries the key and is delighted when it fits the lock. The lock is as rusty as the key, and it takes some effort to turn it. Finally, after much struggling and three turns clockwise, the lock clicks open.

Now Rupert's very pleased to find
That something special lies inside.

He lifts the object out with glee.
"This is the King's crown, certainly!"

The Serpent beams, as if to say,
"That is the King's lost crown. Hurray!"

The Serpent gives the bear a lift,
To make sure that the trip is swift.

Rupert lifts the lid as the Serpent and the Merboy look on eagerly, excited to see what treasures the chest might hold. Inside is a beautiful, ornate, coral crown, sat in a bed of gold coins and glittering jewels of all shapes, sizes and colours. "All this treasure must be worth a small fortune!" Rupert says. "It will certainly cover the storm damage to Sandy Bay!" Rupert lifts the crown out very carefully and studies it in wonder. "It's beautiful!" the Merboy says.

Rupert holds the crown up so the Serpent can see it clearly. "Is this it?" he asks. The Serpent nods happily. "Well, we must get it back to your King," Rupert tells them. "We can take you to him!" the Merboy says. "Let's go!" "Wonderful!" Rupert replies. "But I must tell Sam and Captain Walrus where we're going first." The Serpent pushes Rupert swiftly back up to the surface, towards the boat where Sam and Captain Walrus are waiting.

He holds the crown triumphantly,
And greets his two friends happily.

"I must return it right away,
Then I'll meet you at Sandy Bay."

The Merboy says, "This water flow
Will take us where we want to go."

So jumping on the current, they
Are very quickly whisked away.

Meanwhile, back at the surface, the two men are chatting about fishing conditions when Rupert bursts out of the sea, giving them quite a fright! But they cheer as they see the crown, held triumphantly in Rupert's hand. They haven't spotted the Serpent yet, but then he rises out of the water and they gasp in amazement. "The Serpent and the Merboy are going to take me to the King so I can return the crown," Rupert calls. "There's a treasure chest by the wreck, too!"

"Come back to the bay when you have delivered the crown, I'll wait there for you," Sam promises, then Rupert and the Serpent swim back down towards the wreck, where the Merboy is waiting for them. "Follow me," he says, and leads them to a stretch of water that is flowing more quickly than the rest of the sea – an underwater supercurrent. "Jump on, and it will lead us straight to the King!" he promises. So the three friends jump into the current and are quickly swept away.

Then through an ornate arch they glide
With crab guard pillars at each side.

A light shines up ahead. It's clear
That they are getting very near.

"That must be him, there is no doubt –
The King I've heard so much about."

"Your Majesty, I'm pleased to say,
We found your long-lost crown today."

They float to an ornate doorway, flanked on either side by carved pillars where two crabs are standing guard. They see the crown in Rupert's hand and click their pincers towards the doorway to let them know they are welcome to enter. Swept along by the current, they fly through the arch and into a rocky cave. The cave is gloomy but they can see light up ahead. "We must be getting near!" says Rupert. "The King's chambers are just through there," the Merboy tells him.

Rupert and the Merboy say goodbye to the Serpent, who is simply too large to go any further. Then they head through another archway, into a chamber where the King is sitting in a rocky throne. "Go on!" the Merboy smiles. So Rupert glides forward to introduce himself. "Your Majesty, my name is Rupert Bear. I'm pleased to say that we found your long-lost crown today." He explains about the storm and the chest and holds out the King's crown, for the King to take.

But Rupert looks up in dismay.
The crown seems to dissolve away!

On closer look the bear can see
Small creatures where the crown should be!

The creatures come together, then
They form a crown shape once again.

"I simply can't thank you enough,
Since finding it was surely tough."

The King is overjoyed to see his crown again! But before Rupert can hand it over to him, it begins to dissolve right in front of their eyes. Rupert gasps as it disintegrates and slips through his fingers. "Oh, goodness, what have I done?" he cries, alarmed. "I didn't mean to damage it!" But, as he looks more closely, he sees that the crown is splitting into lots of little creatures. They swim above the King's head and seem to be arranging themselves into a shape.

The creatures slowly reform in the shape of the crown, and settle on the King's head. "Fear not, little bear," the King chuckles. "This is a magical crown, made of lots of coral creatures that can change into different shapes," he explains, admiring his reflection in a mirror. "I simply cannot thank you enough for returning it to me. I imagine it was very difficult to find." "Well, not too difficult," Rupert says. "I had lots of help from the Merboy and the Serpent."

RUPERT RECEIVES A REWARD

"This coral necklace, I declare,
Is your reward, dear Rupert Bear."

The Merboy leads him back up high,
And in a cave they say goodbye.

When Rupert surfaces, it's plain
He's back at Sandy Bay again!

Kind Sam walks Rupert back home, where
He gives the gift to Mrs Bear.

As a reward, the King gives Rupert a beautiful coral necklace. Rupert knows just who to give it to. He thanks the King, and says goodbye, then the Merboy shows Rupert the way out. He leads him along another path back up through the caves until they reach a cave above water, where Rupert can remove his diving helmet. "We could not have done it without you," the Merboy smiles. "Thank you, Rupert!" With a promise to visit the Merboy soon, Rupert waves goodbye.

Emerging from the cave, Rupert finds he is right back where he wants to be, looking out over Sandy Bay. True to his word, Sam is on the beach, waiting for him. "We did it!" Rupert calls as he approaches. "The King has his crown back!" "Well done!" Sam smiles. "You must be exhausted. Let me take you home." So Sam drives Rupert back to his house, and Rupert gives his mummy the necklace, promising to tell her all about his adventures over a nice cup of tea and a slice of cake.

Spot the Difference

Rupert sees lots of beautiful creatures under the sea. There are 10 differences between these two pictures of Rupert swimming through a shoal of fish. Can you spot them all?

Answers: The reeds have disappeared, the key has disappeared, an orange fish has turned yellow, a yellow fish has turned yellow, a green fish has turned blue, more bubbles have appeared, a red fish has turned green, a blue fish has turned green, a red fish has disappeared, Rupert's shoulder strap has turned orange.

RUPERT and the

It's Bonfire Night. The chums all plan
To build the biggest blaze they can.

It is bonfire night and everyone is looking forward to the village firework display. Rupert and his pals are busy gathering wood from the common to add to the blaze. "I wonder what fireworks there will be?" asks Ottoline. "I like pretty ones like Roman candles . . . " "Noisy fireworks are best!" laughs Bill. "I like both," smiles Rupert. "Bodkin told me the Professor has been planning a really special surprise . . . "

Noisy Firework

"What fireworks do you think there'll be?"
"Some noisy ones!" cries Bill with glee.

The old Professor's there to show
Where all the sticks they've found should go.

"Well done!" cries the Professor when he sees how much wood the pals have gathered. "Bodkin can use that to finish building the fire . . . " Handing in their bundles, the chums hurry home for tea, promising to meet up later, as soon as it gets dark. Quite a crowd has gathered by the time the Bears arrive and Rupert can see the Professor waiting to light the fire. "Not long until the fireworks start!" declares Mr Bear.

That evening, Bill and Rupert run
To join the others in the fun.

RUPERT ENJOYS THE FIREWORKS

The bonfire blazes; rockets fly
And showers of bright stars fill the sky.

"Look!" Rupert hears his pal, Bill, yell.
"A noisy rocket! I can tell . . . "

The rocket shoots up overhead,
Then changes colour – blue to red!

It ends up with a bang so loud
It deafens the astonished crowd!

When everyone is gathered round, the Professor lights the bonfire and calls for Bodkin to begin the display. A mighty rocket shoots up into the sky, exploding in a mass of golden star "Beautiful!" sighs Ottoline. "Bravo!" cheers Mr Bear. As Rupert looks on the Professor sets off coloured flares, crackling cascades and a humming saucer. The great bonfire flares up in a tremendous blaze and everyone basks in its glow. "Now for the big surprise!" whispers Bill.

No sooner has Bill spoken than a huge rocket takes off in a streak of silver. Up and up it rises, until it is almost lost from sight. "Gosh!" says Rupert. "It's the biggest firework I've ever seen . . . " Next moment, the rocket explodes in a series of deafening bangs, filling the sky with rainbow-coloured spangles. "Crikey!" gasps Bill. "I thought you liked noise?" laughs Rupert. "What a din!" complains Ottoline. "I'm glad the others weren't like that!"

RUPERT MEETS HORACE HEDGEHOG

"My fault!" the old professor beams.
"I overdid the noise, it seems!"

As everyone is homeward bound
The pals hear a strange rustling sound . . .

It's Horace Hedgehog – wide awake.
"The noise those dreadful fireworks make!"

"I'm meant to hibernate! But how
Can folk sleep with that awful row?"

"I say!" laughs the Professor. "Rather overdid it with that last rocket, I'm afraid! I'd no idea it would be so noisy . . . " Now that the fireworks are over, everyone begins to make their way home. While Mr and Mrs Bear lead the way, Rupert and Bill stop for a final glance at the bonfire. As the pair set off across the common they hear a sudden rustling in a nearby pile of leaves. "What's that?" gasps Bill. "I don't know," says Rupert. "But there's definitely someone there . . . "

As Rupert gets closer, the rustling grows more agitated and a grumpy-looking hedgehog emerges from under the leaves. "Horace!" he cries. "What are you doing here, and why are you wearing a nightcap?" "I'm trying to sleep!" complains Rupert's friend. "Hedgehogs hibernate in the winter, you know. I'd just settled down for a nice long nap when lots of bangs and crashes woke me up . . . " "Oh dear!" says Rupert. "That must have been the firework display."

RUPERT JOINS HIS PALS

"Oh, dear!" says Bill. "I'd no idea
That creatures underground could hear!"

The pals apologise and then
The hedgehog disappears again.

Next morning Rupert's chums call by.
"We're off to play football!" they cry.

The Professor explains that they
Must play their game further away . . .

"Don't be cross," says Bill. "We didn't mean to wake you up. I didn't know you could hear fireworks underground! We'll ask the Professor to make them quieter for next year's display . . . "

"Good!" says Horace. "Now that they've finished, perhaps I can get back to sleep . . . " "Come on, you two!" calls Mr Bear, looking to see where the pals have got to. Rupert turns to wave to Horace but the hedgehog has already disappeared, back to his leafy home.

Next morning Rupert and his pals decide to play football together on the common. "Weren't the fireworks good?" says Rupert. "Yes," agrees Willie. "What a display!" When they reach the common, the chums find the Professor and Bodkin clearing up after last night's fire. "Keep well away!" warns the Professor as Bodkin rakes up the smouldering embers. "Fires can be dangerous, even when they've nearly gone out!" The pals agree to go and play on the far side of the common.

RUPERT SPOTS SOME DAFFODILS

"Goal!" Willie cries, but then, instead,
The ball sails over Rupert's head . . .

As Rupert gets the ball he blinks.
"A daffodil! How odd!" he thinks.

"More daffodils! But why and how?
They grow in early spring, not now!"

"I'll take a bunch back home to show
My parents. Perhaps they might know . . . "

The pals are soon enjoying a lively game, with Rupert taking a turn in goal. "Too high!" he calls as Willie kicks the ball over his head. "Sorry!" cries the little mouse. Rupert runs to get the ball, which has landed behind a clump of bushes. As he bends to pick it up, he suddenly stops and blinks in amazement. "A daffodil!" he gasps. "I didn't know daffodils grew in November. I've only seen them in the spring, when the weather's much milder . . . "

Rupert is about to go back with the football when he suddenly spots a second clump of daffodils, not far from the first. "Look what I've found!" he calls to the others. "Daffodils!" gasps Willie. "It's too cold for flowers. The first sign of frost will finish them off . . . " The chums resume their game of football, but as soon as it ends Rupert decides to pick some daffodils and take them home to show his parents . . .

RUPERT FINDS MORE FLOWERS

*"What lovely daffodils! But where
Did you find them?" gasps Mrs Bear.*

*The flowers leave Mr Bear amazed.
"Perhaps some the Professor's raised?"*

*Next morning Rupert hurries out
To see if more flowers are about . . .*

*"Yes! Tulips too! More over there –
There seem to be bulbs everywhere!"*

Mrs Bear is astonished to see Rupert carrying a bunch of yellow daffodils. "My favourites!" she cries. "But where did you get them?" When she hears how he found them growing on the common, Rupert's mother shakes her head in disbelief. "I've never heard of such a thing!" she exclaims. Mr Bear is puzzled by the daffodils too. "Perhaps they're a special type?" he suggests. "It might be one of the Professor's experiments. But why should he plant them on the common?"

Next day, as soon as he has finished lunch, Rupert decides to go to see if there are any more daffodils growing on the common. He hurries back to the spot where the chums were playing football and searches carefully all around. At first the common seems bare, then he suddenly spots a clump of bright red tulips. "There are more over there!" he marvels. "It looks like a trail of spring bulbs leading over the hill . . ." Excitedly, he runs forward to see where it leads.

RUPERT DISCOVERS AN IMP

"A trail! It leads towards that tree . . . "
Thinks Rupert, looking carefully.

But then he hears a crying sound –
It's one of Nutwood's Imps he's found!

The Imp jumps up and runs away.
"Wait!" Rupert calls. "I'll help you. Stay!"

"I thought spring was your time of year?"
"It is – but I've been stranded here!"

Following the trail of flowers across the common, Rupert finally comes to a large old oak tree. As he gets nearer, he can hear the sound of somebody crying. "I wonder what's wrong?" he thinks and creeps forward to see who is there. To Rupert's surprise, it isn't one of his chums he can hear, but a small figure, dressed in colourful clothes and a pointed hat. "An Imp of Spring!" he murmurs. "But what's an Imp doing here in the middle of winter? And why is he so upset?"

As Rupert steps forward, the little Imp gives a cry of alarm and jumps to his feet. "Hello!" smiles Rupert. "Don't be afraid. I've only come to see what's wrong . . . " "Everything!" sobs the Imp. "It's cold and damp and not at all like spring. I ought to be tucked up in a nice warm bed . . . " "I know!" says Rupert. "I thought you all stayed underground until winter ended?" "We do!" sniffs the miserable Imp. "I came out early to look at something and now I can't get back . . . "

RUPERT HEARS THE IMP'S TALE

The Imp was sleeping underground,
When suddenly, he heard a sound . . .

"I didn't know what it could be
So dressed and came outside to see . . . "

"The coloured lights I saw were so
Enchanting that I couldn't go!"

"At last I hurried home once more
But found a wind had shut the door!"

"It all started when a noisy bang woke me up," explains the Imp. "Everyone else was still sound asleep but I thought I'd go and see what was happening. It was dark when I stepped outside, the sky was full of flashing lights, and a crowd had gathered on the far side of the common." "The fireworks!" says Rupert. "So that's what they're called!" cries the Imp. "They were so pretty I decided to stay and watch. I couldn't resist leaving the tree and having a closer look . . . "

The Imp tells Rupert that he saw everyone gathered together round a great big fire. "It was cold on the common," he explains, "so I came as close as I could to try and keep warm. As soon as the fireworks ended I hurried back to the hollow tree, only to find that the door had blown shut. I couldn't get it open again, no matter how I tried. The others are all sleeping, so no-one can let me in. It's too chilly to stay out any longer, but I just don't know what else to do . . . "

RUPERT TAKES THE IMP HOME

*"I can't undo the hidden lock
And nobody will hear us knock!"*

*"It's far too cold for you to stay
Out here! Come back with me. This way . . . "*

*"Poor thing!" says Mrs Bear. "Eat these!
And stay for as long as you please."*

*They put the Imp to bed. "Good night!
We'll talk tomorrow, when it's light."*

Rupert tries knocking at the door in the tree but receives no reply . . . "Are there other entrances to Imp Headquarters?" he asks. "Yes," says the Imp. "But everything's been shut up for the winter!" "You can't stay out here in the cold!" says Rupert. "Why don't you come home with me?" Wrapping the shivering Imp in his scarf, he leads the way across the common towards the lights of Nutwood. "That's my house," he smiles. "Come in and warm up while we work out what to do next . . . "

Mrs Bear is amazed to see the little Imp. "I expect you're hungry!" she says when she hears what has happened. "I hope Imps like chocolate biscuits . . . " As they chat by the fire, the Imp tells Rupert that his name is Willow. "I've never been in a house before!" he smiles. "Time you were off to sleep now," says Rupert's mother. "You must be very tired." "Goodnight!" waves Rupert as the Imp settles down. "Tomorrow we'll find a way back to your home . . . "

RUPERT KNOWS THE ANSWER

Next morning, Rupert says that he
Knows someone they should go and see . . .

The Imp thanks Mrs Bear, then they
Set off together, straightaway.

"It's Horace! He'll know what to do!
He hibernates in winter too . . . "

The hedgehog's fast asleep as well.
"I hope that he can hear the bell!"

Next morning Willow has his first taste of toast and marmalade as he joins the Bears for breakfast. "It's very kind of you to look after me," he smiles, "but I can't stay here all winter!" "There must be another way back to Imp Headquarters," declares Rupert, then suddenly he has a good idea. "I know somebody we can ask to help us!" he cries. "We'll go and see them as soon as you've finished . . . " "Good luck!" calls Mrs Bear as the pair set off towards the common.

"Who are we going to see?" asks Willow. "Horace Hedgehog!" laughs Rupert. "He lives underground too . . . " Explaining how Horace was woken by the noise of the fireworks, Rupert pushes aside a pile of old leaves and squeezes through a gap in the tree's roots. Scrambling down a flight of steps, he finds a small wooden door with a bell-pull outside. "Do you think he'll hear?" asks Willow. "I don't know," says Rupert. "Let's hope he doesn't sleep too heavily . . . "

The door swings open slowly, then
Horace groans, "No! Not you again . . ."

"I'm sorry!" Rupert says. "But we
Need help! It's an emergency . . ."

As soon as Horace hears what's wrong
He says he'll help. "It won't take long!"

He sets off down a corridor
The Imp has never seen before.

For a long time nothing happens, then Rupert hears the door start to open . . . "Who's there?" calls Horace. "You again!" he gasps. "What do you mean by waking me up for a second time?" "I'm sorry," says Rupert, "but my friend's in trouble and you're the only one who might be able to help . . ." "An Imp!" blinks the hedgehog. "What's he doing out at this time of year? He ought to be in bed!" "That's what's wrong," says Rupert and quickly explains how Willow was stranded . . .

When Horace hears Willow's story, he soon agrees to help the Imp. "We must have both been woken by the same rocket!" he smiles. "You were right to come and see me, Rupert. I do know an entrance to Imp Headquarters, although it's hardly ever used." Telling the pair to follow him closely, Horace sets off along a gloomy corridor that passes by his leafy winter chambers. "I'm afraid it's rather narrow at first," he tells Rupert. "But you'll soon be able to stand up properly . . ."

RUPERT FOLLOWS THE MAP

"It leads out to a path I share
With Elves and Imps," he tells the pair.

"That's marvellous!" the lost Imp cries.
"This tunnel's one I recognise!"

"Look! There's a sign!" he cries with glee.
"This way, Rupert! Just follow me . . . "

Another sign. The Imps' H.Q.
"We have to go through this door too!"

At the far end of the corridor, Horace unlocks another door to reveal a well-lit passageway. "You should recognise where you are now," he tells Willow. Sure enough, the little Imp gives a cry of delight as he steps out into the light. "It's one of our main paths!" he laughs. "I've often been this way, but I never knew anyone else lived here!" "Off you go," smiles Horace. "I'm going back to bed now and this time I'm not getting up until Spring has arrived . . . "

Willow is so pleased to be back underground that he scampers along, leaving Rupert far behind. "Wait for me!" he calls, hurrying to catch up. "Sorry!" laughs the Imp. "There isn't much further to go now. All we have to do is follow the signs . . . " "Do you ever get lost?" asks Rupert. "Sometimes," admits Willow. "The best thing then is to pop up and have a look above ground." Reaching another door, he pushes it open and beckons for Rupert to follow . . .

RUPERT SEES A DORMITORY

"Quiet now!" the Imp warns. "Not a peep!
The others should be fast asleep . . . "

"Thank goodness! No-one saw me go.
Now nobody need ever know!"

The Imp yawns as he dons his cap.
"Now I'll resume my winter nap!"

He thanks Rupert and then declares,
"The way home's up that flight of stairs!"

As they enter Imp Headquarters, Rupert notices the lights growing dimmer. "We're nearly at the Dormitory now," whispers Willow. "Try not to make any noise . . . " He pulls aside a heavy curtain and Rupert hears a gentle snoring sound coming from within. Creeping forward he sees a long room lined with hundreds of beds, each of which contains a peacefully-slumbering Imp. "No-one else is awake!" says Willow. "With a bit of luck, they'll never know I've been outside . . . "

Now that he is back in the Dormitory, Willow soon feels drowsy. "I'm glad I saw the fireworks," he yawns, "but there's nothing I'd like better than a nice long nap . . . " "Perhaps you can visit us again when winter's over?" says Rupert. "You'll always be welcome to come to tea . . . " "Thank you," says the Imp. "And thanks for all your help!" Out in the corridor, he points to a steep flight of steps. "That's the way to Nutwood," he smiles. "Just keep climbing up . . . "

The winding staircase seems to stop
Abruptly as he nears the top!

Then, opening a little door,
He finds himself outside once more . . .

Nearby stands Bill and Ottoline.
They've no idea where Rupert's been!

"What lovely blooms!" Ottoline cries.
"The last till spring!" Rupert replies.

Waving goodbye to his new friend, Rupert clambers up the winding staircase. Before long, he finds himself surrounded by a tangle of roots, which gets thicker and thicker the further he goes. At last he reaches what seems to be a dead-end. "It must be a door!" he thinks and pushes against it with all his might. Suddenly, he finds himself back on Nutwood Common, where he first met Willow. "If only the others were here," he smiles. "Imagine how surprised they'd be!"

No sooner has Rupert closed the door in the tree than he spots Ottoline and Bill, following the trail of tulips and daffodils. "Hello!" calls Ottoline. "Aren't these flowers lovely!" "Rupert found them yesterday," laughs Bill, "when we were out playing football . . ." "Are there any more?" she asks. "No!" smiles Rupert, thinking of the sleeping Imps. "I'm sure that's the last of them. We won't see any more daffodils now until the start of spring . . ."

Rupert's Baby Rabbit

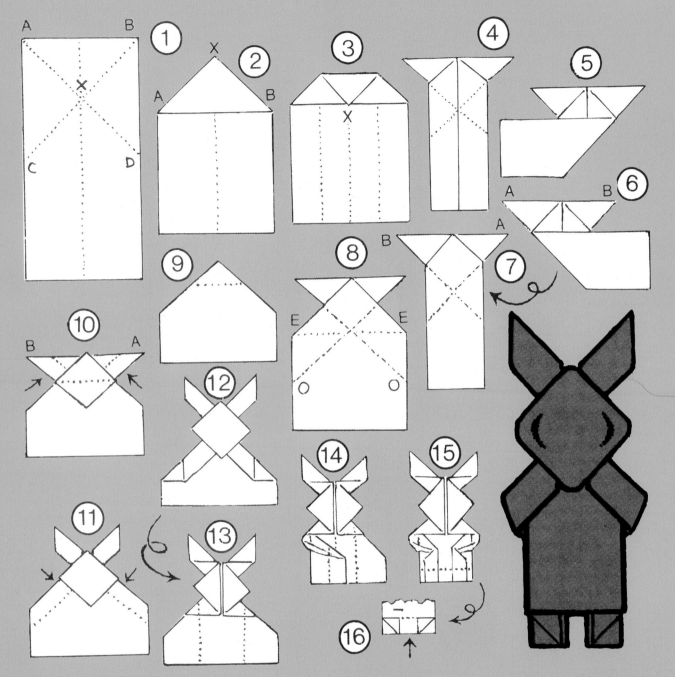

This clever paperfold of the Rabbit brothers' little sister was devised by Thea Clift. You will need a piece of thin paper twice as high as it is wide. Fold it up the middle. Lay the top edge against each side in turn to make the creases shown in (1), meeting at X. Bring upper sides together so that AB comes down to CD (2) and fold X to the middle of AB (3). Carefully fold both sides to middle, starting at bottom. As you go up lift X and AB so that X disappears behind and you get 4. Using new dotted lines lift lower half of paper and lay it across each way (5,6). Press creases firmly. Turn over (7). Open out paper from behind (8) far enough to complete the sloping creases to O and O. Use these creases to press angles E and E back and down.

The top half will fold back leaving 9. Fold down top point bringing back X and AB (10). Fold up arrowed sides along new dotted lines to form ears – note the hidden extra thickness which must be folded – (11). Do the same with other arrowed sides to make (12). Turn over (13). Use one dotted line to take one short side across beyond middle line (14). Fold it back again nearly to outer edge. Repeat with other short side to make (15). Turn up bottom edge to make last dotted line. Straighten and turn over. Fold up both the lowest corners (16). Press single thickness (arrowed) back and tuck up out of sight. Draw the eyes well to the side of the head. Turn back a trifle of each point on the head to make them rounder.

REST AT TOP OF STEPS MISS ONE TURN

GO FORWARD TO NO. 26

28

23

FEEL GIDDY GO BACK TO NO. 24 AND MISS ONE TURN

27

22

24

25

26

21

GO BACK TO NO. 16

20

TAKE A SHORT CUT TO NO. 24

19

18

GO BACK TO NO. 3 TO PICK UP YOUR HANDKERCHIEF

MISS YOUR FOOTING SLIDE BACK TO NO. 14

9

17

16

8

15

FALL IN THE RIVER START AGAIN FROM NO. 1

10

14

12

11

JUMP TO NO. 13

7

13

TAKE ONE EXTRA TURN

6

3

JUMP TO NO. 7

5

2

4

START

1

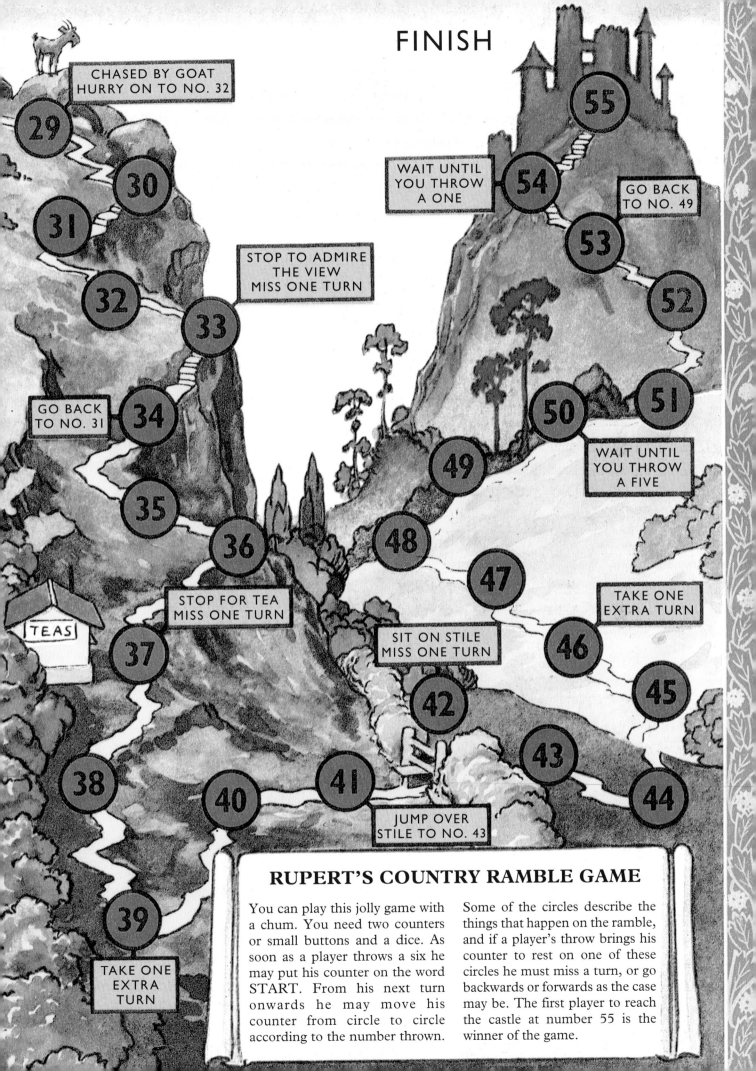

FINISH

CHASED BY GOAT
HURRY ON TO NO. 32

29

30

31

32

33

STOP TO ADMIRE
THE VIEW
MISS ONE TURN

GO BACK
TO NO. 31

34

35

36

TEAS

37

STOP FOR TEA
MISS ONE TURN

38

39

TAKE ONE
EXTRA
TURN

40

41

JUMP OVER
STILE TO NO. 43

42

SIT ON STILE
MISS ONE TURN

43

44

45

46

TAKE ONE
EXTRA TURN

47

48

49

50

51

WAIT UNTIL
YOU THROW
A FIVE

52

53

GO BACK
TO NO. 49

54

WAIT UNTIL
YOU THROW
A ONE

55

RUPERT'S COUNTRY RAMBLE GAME

You can play this jolly game with a chum. You need two counters or small buttons and a dice. As soon as a player throws a six he may put his counter on the word START. From his next turn onwards he may move his counter from circle to circle according to the number thrown.

Some of the circles describe the things that happen on the ramble, and if a player's throw brings his counter to rest on one of these circles he must miss a turn, or go backwards or forwards as the case may be. The first player to reach the castle at number 55 is the winner of the game.

RUPERT
and the
CARVED STICK

Its long-hidden secret lies in a jumble of words and numbers. Even the owner cannot understand the message until by a lucky chance Rupert and Edward find the first clue. Then what an exciting search begins!

RUPERT HEARS A RATTLING NOISE

"Oh, Daddy's busy I can see,
He has no time to talk to me."

"Hark, Mummy! What's that rattling sound?"
Asks Rupert, turning sharply round.

He runs outside, then has a shock,
That car looks like a real old crock!

"Just look what's standing in our lane!"
Cries Rupert, dashing back again.

"DADDY seems very quiet this morning," thinks Rupert as he watches Mr Bear surrounded by sheets of paper which he reads slowly one by one before tearing them up. "I wonder where he got all those papers from. Some of them have pictures of pretty places on them." Finding himself unnoticed he wanders into the kitchen to ask his mummy. "You'll learn in good time," she murmurs. All at once a rattling noise makes him turn and listen. The sound continues, and Rupert loses no time in going outside to find what is causing it. Standing in the road, with its engine still running, is one of the funniest little old cars he has ever seen. A mechanic beside it switches off the engine and moves forward. "Does Mr Bear live here? This is for him," he says. "Y-yes, I'll go and fetch him," gasps Rupert in excitement. But to his astonishment Mr and Mrs Bear show no surprise at what he tells them so excitedly about the funny car.

RUPERT LOOKS AT THE CAR

"That car's for us," his daddy says,
"I've hired it for the holidays."

The quaint old car looks spick and span.
"It's in good order," says the man.

Next day, they plan a picnic treat,
Smiles Mummy, "Yes, there's one spare seat."

So Rupert sets off at a run,
To find a pal to share the fun.

Seeing Rupert's puzzled expression Mr Bear chuckles cheerfully. "I'd better explain," he says. "We've been worrying about holidays. I've looked at all sorts of advertisements, and we can't afford any of the places they speak about, so I've found an old car that we can hire cheaply rund we'll make some nice day trips from here. Come along, let's look at it." Rupert needs no second bidding, and they both hurry out to get instructions from the waiting mechanic.

The next morning is sunny, and Rupert gets up early to ask if they can go on their first holiday trip, but his mummy has already had the same idea, and is busy packing a case with good things for a picnic. "What fun it's going to be," he exclaims. "I wish we could take one of my pals. Would that car hold another?" "Yes, just one, I expect," says Mrs Bear. "Only you must hurry. Ask the very first pal you meet." So after breakfast Rupert runs outside to see which of the pals is around.

RUPERT INVITES EDWARD TRUNK

*"Oh dear," he sighs. "I haven't met
A single friend to join us yet."*

*Then Edward Trunk comes up the rise,
"A picnic? Yes – I'll come!" he cries.*

*"My brother Pompey's very small,
He won't take any room at all."*

*"Hello," calls Rupert, "here we are!
I hope we'll all fit in the car."*

For a few minutes Rupert wanders about keeping a sharp look-out for his pals. "Where are they today?" he murmurs. "Perhaps I'd better call at the cottage of one of them." At that moment there is a cheery call from behind a bush and Edward Trunk appears pushing his baby brother Pompey. "Hello, Edward, you're in luck," Rupert smiles. "We're going for a picnic in a little old car, and Mummy says I may bring the first pal I meet. Well, that's you! Would you like to come with us and share the fun?" Edward is delighted at the invitation. "What, come for a picnic with you!" he cries. "That would be topping. My people have left me to take care of Pompey all day and I've been wondering what to do with him." "Oh dear, that's different!" says Rupert doubtfully. "My mummy said that I could take one pal and Pompey would make two. Never mind, let's go and see if the car's strong enough." So the little procession makes its way over the grass

RUPERT REACHES THE SEA

Excitedly they all climb in,
The engine pops – and off they spin.

Some pals are playing on the grass
And cheer to see the strange sight pass.

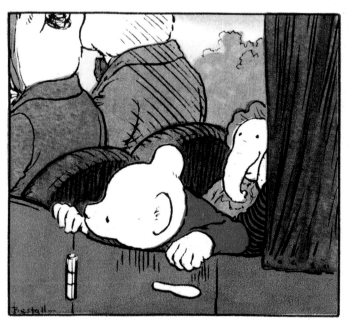

They travel at a steady pace,
Till Rupert calls, "Here's just the place!"

"A ruined castle by the sea!"
Shouts Rupert's pal excitedly.

Mr Bear is even more doubtful than Rupert about taking so many on his first trip in the ancient car, but at length he agrees. "It will give the machine a good trial and I must go slowly," he says. "Pompey's folding chair can go under your feet with the case of picnic food." Soon they are all fitted in, the engine gives one or two pops and sneezes, then it starts, and some more of Rupert's pals turn up to cheer them as they rattle away into the country for their picnic. The little friends are now all agog. "Where are you going to take us, Daddy?" asks Rupert. "I don't exactly know," replies Mr Bear. "We can't make plans until we are sure that this funny little car will hold out. Let's just keep going." So they jog quietly along side roads until Rupert gives a happy shout. "Look, look, there's the sea right beside us!" "Yes, and there's a lovely ruined castle! Can't we stop here?" calls Edward. And so Mr Bear puts on the brake and they get out.

60

RUPERT BEGINS TO EXPLORE

They all decide they'd like to stay,
Then start their picnic straight away.

Says Mummy, "Yes, you may explore,
And take a walk along the shore."

The chums stroll on, until they spy
A rocky island, steep and high.

"Well, Edward, we can't get there now!
But here's the castle, anyhow."

Mr Bear is relieved at having driven so far without trouble, and while Mrs Bear is setting out the picnic he takes the little car off the road and on to the grass. Edward is now getting wildly excited. "I've never been inside a ruined castle in my life!" he declares. "Will it be full of buried treasure? May Rupert and I go exploring?" Mrs Bear smiles. "Yes, if you're very careful," she says, "though you'd better leave Pompey with us." So after a good meal the two pals scamper away together.

Rupert and Edward push their way through the bushes and over the great blocks of fallen stonework until quite suddenly they find themselves in an open space with the sea before them. "Oo, what a grand little island that is!" cries Rupert. "It looks jolly difficult to climb." "I wish we could try," says Edward. "How do we get there?" "We don't," laughs Rupert. "There isn't time." He leads the way back, but Edward still casts wistful looks at the island.

They make their way through broken walls,
And archways dim, where ivy falls.

Then Edward who is peering round,
Calls out, "Hi! Look what I have found!"

The stick is carved from end to end.
"How odd!" says Rupert to his friend.

A set of numbers can be seen,
And thirteen words! What do they mean?

Edward still wants to stand gazing at the island, and Rupert wonders how to get him away from the edge of the cliff. "Come on," he calls. "Don't you want to explore the ruined castle? You said there might be buried treasure here." At that his pal hurries to join him, and they have fun clambering over the broken walls and into mossy hollows. All at once Rupert hears his name being called. "Hi, come back a minute," Edward sounds urgent. "Look what I've found." Joining his friend, Rupert finds him peering at a waking-stick leaning against a wall. "Hello, it seems as if there is somebody else here," he says. "No one would go away and forget a fine stick like that. See, it's carved all over, beautifully carved. There are words all down the stick." "Yes, and even the handle has something carved on it," says Edward. "What is it?" "It's a set of numbers, in this order: '7326514'," murmurs Rupert. "What do you think they mean?"

RUPERT TELLS THE STRANGER

Just then, the two chums jump apart,
As heavy footsteps make them start.

"Ahem! That walking-stick is mine!
Look at the carvings – aren't they fine?"

"Oh, do explain them," Rupert pleads.
So from his stick the stranger reads:

"Highest-rock-shall-give-to-oak
The-point-line-and-the-silver-oak."

The two pals look at the odd row of figures on the handle. "What can '7326514' mean?" mutters Edward. "It isn't a year and it can't be somebody's age." As they move along, a stern voice interrupts their thoughts. "Well, and what may you two be doing here?" A solemn-looking gentleman is facing them among the fallen stones. "Oh, please, we're on a picnic and we're exploring this old castle," says Rupert, "and we've just found this strange walking-stick with carvings on it. Is it yours?" The gentleman's expression slowly softens. "Yes, that's my stick," he says. "I found it recently among the old family things." "I think it's lovely," says Rupert, "but what do all those carved words and numbers mean?" "I can't imagine," laughs the man. "They're very odd. Let's read the words. They say, 'Highest-rock-shall-give-to-oak-the-point-line-and-the-silver-oak!'" "Surely that doesn't mean anything!" exclaims Edward. "It's nonsense."

"Just what that means I cannot tell!
There are some figures here as well."

Then Rupert, as he turns to go,
Hears Edward ask, "I'd like to know . . . "

"This castle's mine. And once, they say,
Rare silver things were stored away."

"My nephews hope to find it all,
They're digging now beside that wall."

For some minutes the gentleman muses over the words carved along the stick. "I've puzzled over this quite a bit," he murmurs. "Those words, 'Highest rock shall give to oak the point line and the silver oak' must mean something, but what? And why the figures '7326514' on the handle? Perhaps the man who carved them was practising without meaning anything!" Rupert thinks it is time to go, but Edward hangs back as if there is something he wants to say. After a pause he asks breathlessly, "Please, is this lovely ruined castle yours? And is there lots of buried treasure here?" Rupert laughs, but the gentleman doesn't. "It's odd that you should ask that," he says. "Yes, this castle is mine and there is an ancient story that some rare and wonderful silver was buried here in the bad old days. We've searched nearly everywhere, and look, there are two of my nephews, who still feel hopeful, and they're still digging for it in my grounds!"

RUPERT HAS A BIG SHOCK

Still thinking of the mystery,
They stand and gaze across the sea.

"Oo-oh!" exclaims the startled man,
And saves himself as best he can.

"Dear me," he sighs, "my stick is lost!
It must be found at any cost."

"May we search first?" the two chums ask.
"Your nephews need not leave their task."

The gentleman knows nothing more about the buried silver so he wanders away towards the cliff. "That rocky island looks topping," says Rupert. "I wish we could go there and climb." "H'm, perhaps some day, though it's difficult," the gentleman smiles. "There's only one place to land and . . . " At that moment there is a slight noise behind him and without warning a piece of the cliff edge gives way. He lurches forward to save himself, but, without thinking, he lets go of the precious carved stick. In his relief at saving himself from such a fall, the gentleman doesn't appear to notice what has happened to his stick until Rupert tells him that it has gone right down the cliff. "Oh my, I don't want to lose it. It has been in my family for a long time," he exclaims. He kneels as near the edge as he dare, then he turns to fetch help. "Would you let us try to find it?" asks Rupert. "Yes," adds Edward. "The tide might carry it away."

"All right, but don't go near the brink,
This is a safer way, I think."

The chums descend a rocky slope,
They'll find the stick quite soon, they hope.

"These rocks will make it very hard,
We'll have to search them yard by yard."

"I say!" calls Rupert, turning back,
"The stick has fallen down a crack!"

The gentleman hesitates. "Yes, it is important to get that old walking-stick back as quickly as we can," he says. "You may try if you like, and if you don't find it at once I'll fetch my nephews. Hi, come away from the edge, you know how dangerous it is. There's a much better way down over here." For Rupert and Edward are peering down the cliff hoping to see the missing stick. Now they follow the way that is pointed out, and it leads them down a very rough boulder-strewn pathway.

At length the two pals arrive at the foot of the cliffs and are quite near the sea. "I say, this is a strange sort of shore, isn't it?" says Rupert. "There's no beach or sand and only these great lumps of rock. It'll be slow work climbing over them, and the stick could be hidden anywhere in these deep cracks. I wonder which bit of cliff it fell down." Edward pauses to shout the question to the old gentleman at the cliff-top. Suddenly there is a happy cry from Rupert.

RUPERT TUGS HIS HARDEST

*"How lucky that it's stayed upright!
It could have fallen out of sight."*

*But now they find the stick won't move,
They cannot shift it from that groove.*

*"The handle's jammed! But wait a bit!
The end can be unscrewed from it!"*

*"We cannot stop to wonder why,"
Says Edward. "Let me have a try."*

Scrambling forward as fast as he can to see what has caused his pal so much excitement, Edward finds Rupert gazing at something between two boulders. "Look here," the little bear calls. "The carved stick has bounced and landed here. What a bit of luck that it remained on end. If it had settled in the crack between those rocks we should never have found it! The handle's jammed down between those rocks. Let's pull it out. My, it's tightly fixed!" He tugs and twists this way and that, but cannot free the stick. All at once something seems to give way. "Oh! Have you broken it?" gasps Edward. "No, I believe it's unscrewing!" mutters Rupert. Next instant he holds up a small object. "See, it's the end piece of the stick," he whispers. "It has the one word 'OAK' carved on it, the last word of that jumbled sentence. I wonder if the gentleman knows that it unscrews. And that the stick is divided into sections. Shall we try unscrewing the others?"

RUPERT CLIMBS TO THE TOP

A push from Edward does the trick,
And frees the quaint old walking-stick.

"Now, watch your step! This part's the worst,"
Puffs Rupert Bear. "Let me go first."

"We've found your stick! The end unscrews!"
Cries Rupert, quick to tell his news.

"H'm, that will screw back in again,
But what it's for I can't explain."

Edward doesn't think that Rupert's idea is at all a good one. "Even if you did unscrew all the sections of the stick the handle would be jammed," he says. "It only needs a tiny movement of one of those rocks and you could lift the stick out. Here, let me try." With his feet against one of the boulders and his back against another he pushes hard. "That's done it," cries Rupert. "Whew, it's lucky you came on this outing. You're the strongest of all my pals!" And they climb back up the steep rocky path. At the top of the cliff Rupert hands over the precious carved stick, and the gentleman gazes in astonishment at the separate end section. "This was certainly meant to be screwed in," he murmurs thoughtfully. "How beautifully it is made. There are seven sections altogether. Perhaps the clever carver who made the stick found it easier to put his carving on to each section separately before screwing them together. Little bear, this is a discovery!"

RUPERT HURRIES WITH EDWARD

"He's deep in thought, we need not wait,"
Says Edward. "And it's getting late."

Gasps Rupert, "Yes, we quite forgot,
We're due back at the picnic spot!"

Then Rupert hears an urgent shout,
He knows that voice, without a doubt.

"Please wait!" the gentleman exclaims,
"I quite forgot to ask your names!"

The curious thing that has happened to the carved stick seems to set the gentleman's thoughts in a new direction and he sits down staring at it intently. At the long silence the two pals grow restive. "If the stick's all right I ought to be going now," says Rupert politely. "Yes, and I must go and see how my little brother Pompey is getting on," adds Edward. They say goodbye, but the gentleman doesn't appear to hear them and is too absorbed to notice as they hurry back through the ruins of the castle. Running between the great fallen stones and keeping the sea on their left, the two pals return to their starting point only to find that Mr and Mrs Bear have packed up the picnic things. "There's my Pompey and he looks all right," Edward puffs. "Sorry we've been so long." Rupert close behind him, hears another sound. "Wait a moment! Somebody's calling," he says. Turing back after a few paces he sees that the gentleman is following them.

RUPERT ASKS HIS MUMMY

"We've never met, I must confess,
But may I know your home address?"

"Your story will take quite a time,"
Says Mrs Bear. "So in you climb!"

"I hope he'll call, just like he said,"
Smiles Rupert, when he's tucked in bed.

"Now who would knock so early on?"
Asks Mrs Bear. "The postman's gone."

The gentleman joins Rupert. "I was hoping to catch you up," he says. "Ah, good day, Sir," he adds, facing the surprised Mr Bear. "These young people have been so useful that I hope to meet them again. May I know your address?" Mr Bear tells him that it is in Nutwood village and when the gentleman has made his departure, he asks Rupert for the story, but it takes so long that he makes everyone pile into the rattly little car and the long tale has to be finished after they have arrived safely home. Rupert is still full of the mystery of the carved stick when bedtime comes. "I can remember it all clearly, Mummy," he declares. "Right down the stick were the words 'Highest rock shall give to oak the point line and the sliver oak'. What is a silver oak?" "I have no idea," says Mrs Bear. "Unless the silver is buried under an oak. Now you must go to sleep." Next morning at breakfast Rupert is asking his daddy the same question when there is a knock at the door.

RUPERT IS EAGER TO START

When Mummy hurries to the door,
They see the gentleman once more.

"Please, Mrs Bear, would you allow
Your son to journey with me now?"

The gentleman takes Rupert's hand,
And tells him, "You'll soon understand."

"Hullo again! It's nice to meet!"
Beams Edward, perched upon the seat.

Mrs Bear opens the cottage door and on hearing another voice Rupert runs to join her. Their friend of yesterday is standing there. "Good morning," he says, and there is something urgent in his voice. "I've come to collect those two young people who were with me yesterday. I think I have something very interesting to show them." "I don't know if our funny little car is ready," says Mrs Bear. "I have something faster than that!" the gentleman smiles as he points to a large, shiny car standing not far away. After some hesitation Mrs Bear gives her permission for Rupert to go with their new friend. "What are you going to show us?" asks the little bear eagerly. "Have you found the missing silver? Is it something to do with the carved stick? Are we going straight across to fetch Edward?" "Here, not so many questions!" laughs the gentleman. And when the car is opened, Rupert sees that Edward is already there.

RUPERT ARRIVES AT A HOUSE

"I'm glad you both enjoyed your ride,
But, come! We must go straight inside."

The gentleman strides through his hall,
"This way!" the two chums hear him call.

"The sections of my stick must be
Arranged another way," says he.

"The figures on the handle show
Just in which order they should go."

Rupert and Edward are thrilled at travelling in such a fast, smooth car. "Fancy being in our rickety old car yesterday and now in such a wonderful one," laughs Rupert. "Riding in this one is like being in bed." When they finally stop they spend so long admiring the glossy car that the gentleman has to call them, and they follow him into his large house wondering what has made him so excited and what he has to show them. Inside the house the gentleman produces the carved stick. "I do believe I've discovered its message!" he says excitedly and, moving into another room, he finds pencil and paper. "Now then, what are those figures on the handle?" "They are '7326514'," answers Rupert. "Yes," says the gentleman. "Seven figures, and there are seven sections on the stick. You yourself found that the seventh section has the word 'oak' on it. That leaves twelve words carved on the other six sections, or two words to each of them."

RUPERT READS THE MESSAGE

"So in that order we must place
The strange words carved within each space."

"Just listen, while I read them out!"
Laughs Rupert, capering about.

When Rupert Bear has read the line,
He says, "It makes sense now! That's fine!"

"Indeed it is," the man agrees,
And goes to find the two oak trees.

Rupert gets as excited as the gentleman as he begins to get the idea. "Please may I take a pencil and work it out?" he begs. "I'm going to put the sections of the stick in the order of the figures on the handle. Look, section seven has the single word 'oak' on it. Section three has two words 'to oak'. Section two has the words 'shall give'." Writing very clearly and carefully, he puts down all the carved words in their new order, gazes at them for a moment, and then dances round the room gleefully waving the paper. At length Edward becomes impatient. "Stop prancing about and let's hear what you've written!" he laughs. "Right," says Rupert. "My message from the stick reads: 'Oak to oak shall give the silver line and highest rock the point'. It sounds like sense, though I still can't understand it." "But I can!" cries the gentleman. "I worked out the message too, and I believe it will lead us to my buried silver! Let's try." And they hurry out.

RUPERT WAITS ON A STUMP

"I cannot see a single oak,"
Sighs Rupert. "It must be a joke."

"This was an oak! So up you jump,
While Edward mounts the other stump."

But when they scan the line between,
There is no high rock to be seen.

Then Rupert shouts, "Just come back here!
You'll find the answer's very clear!"

Amid the ruins the gentleman pauses for the two pals to catch up. "Please, why does the message speak about oaks?" Rupert asks. "I haven't seen any oaks here." "No, but there were two very old ones," says the gentleman. "They would have been flourishing when the stick was carved, though only their stumps remain now. Look, here is one. You stand on it and I'll take your friend over to the other. Then we'll see if the line from oak to oak really does lead to that precious buried silver!" As he stands Edward on the stump of the other oak the gentleman quietly repeats the message from the stick. "'Oak to oak shall give the silver line and highest rock the point'. Well, here's the line from oak to oak. The end of the message must mean that the highest rock on that line marks the point where the silver is to be found. But there isn't any high rock at all. Only grass and smallish stones and trees beyond." As he finishes there is a loud shout from Rupert.

RUPERT SOLVES THE PUZZLE

The gentleman makes Edward wait,
While he goes to investigate.

"A line from oak to oak would run
Straight to that rock lit by the sun."

"You must be right!" the old man smiles.
"That is the highest rock for miles."

"Come on," he urges, running fast.
"We've solved the mystery at last!"

Leaving Edward on one tree stump the gentleman trots over to Rupert on the other. "What is it, little bear?" he asks gloomily. "I can't get any sense out of that message from the stick. The line shows nothing but grass and trees." "But surely you were looking at it from the wrong end!" cries Rupert. "Stand back and look at the other oak and see where the line leads you." The gentleman follows his pointing finger and gives a start. "The island! My island!" he gasps in astonishment. After the excitement of Rupert's discovery the gentleman becomes brisk and alert again. "You're right! You must be right!" he exclaims. "The island is mine. It has always been part of the castle estate. And it's rock, solid rock. See how high it is! This good old carved stick has given up its secret at last! Come on, my nephews are away today. We must go ourselves." He hurries towards a path to the beach while Rupert and Edward follow.

RUPERT GOES TO AN ISLAND

He hurries off across the sands,
To where his private boat-house stands.

With Edward using all his strength,
They get the craft afloat at length.

The island, as they come in range,
Looks very desolate and strange.

"Just pull the boat up to that cleft,
And then it can be safely left."

While they are scrambling down another steep cliff path after the gentleman Rupert tells Edward what has happened. "The line from oak to oak that the carved stick called the 'silver line' leads straight to the island," he explains. "You said you were longing to visit the island and now it looks as though you'll get there sooner than you expected." Leading the way to a boat-house, the gentleman pulls out a neat little craft and they all help to haul it down to the edge of the water.

After a lot of pushing by Edward the boat has its prow in the water, the oars are fetched, the two pals are put on board and off they go. "I do hope the island is as exciting as it looked when we first saw it," says Rupert. The sea is quite calm and they make good progress. "There's only one tiny beach where we can land," says the gentleman as he rows towards the rugged cliffs. Soon the boat is grating on a narrow stretch of pebbles and Rupert jumps out to help pull it in.

RUPERT FINDS A FLAT ROCK

"I've left my stick and cannot climb!
We'll have to search another time."

"But we can climb up on our own,"
Cries Rupert, starting off alone.

"This rock is on the highest peak,
I'm sure it is the point we seek!"

"We've found the point," says Rupert Bear,
"The silver must be here – but where?"

When the boat is secured and all three have landed, the gentleman makes a gesture of annoyance. "Tcha! How careless of me!" he grumbles. "In my excitement I've left that stick behind in the boat-house. Without it I can't climb up and down these steep cliffs." But Rupert is keen to push on. "Won't you let Edward and me go up alone?" he begs. "Well, all right. I used to manage it when I was young, so I expect you can, although it's difficult," says the gentleman.

The pals are soon scrambling upward. Rupert enjoys the climb so much that Edward is left toiling behind him, but at length they are over the worst of it and come to grass slopes leading to a flattish rock at the very top of the island. "Here it is!" cries Rupert. "The carved stick said that the highest rock gives the point where the silver is hidden!" "Yes, but where is it hidden?" says Edward breathlessly. "There's not a sign of any hiding place."

RUPERT IS SHOWN A CLUE

Then Edward calls, "Hi, not so quick!
This mark is like the walking-stick."

"Perhaps the carving is a clue,"
Breathes Rupert. "What's it pointing to?"

Cries Edward, "Here's a mystery!
It only points straight out to sea!"

"No," Rupert frowns. "It can't mean that,
This stone is what it's pointing at."

After searching all round the rough top of the island without success, Rupert thinks they ought to return and then moves off. To his surprise his pal does not follow. "Hi, wait a bit," calls Edward. "I believe I've found a clue!" Hurrying back, Rupert finds him gazing at something on the surface of the highest rock. "Something was carved there long ago," says Edward softly. "It's full of moss now, but d'you see what it is? It's just the shape of that carved stick!" Rupert quickly catches Edward's excitement. "We must be on the right trail!" he exclaims. "It can't be just chance that a carving looking just like the carved wooden stick is up here." "Well, but what now?" says Edward. He stands on the rock and stares in the direction that the stick is pointing. "There's nothing but the open sea out there," he mutters. "Perhaps it's pointing at something much nearer," says Rupert. "What about this boulder jammed against the rock?"

Though Edward tries, and tries again,
The boulder will not budge, it's plain.

"I think the gentleman should know,"
Says Rupert, and he turns to go.

But Edward Trunk will not give in,
"No, wait," he puffs, "I mean to win!"

At last, the boulder starts to roll,
And brings to light a gaping hole.

Edward cheers up at Rupert's words. "Yes, that boulder's not too big," he says. "Let's see if it will move. It may be hiding the secret. There seems to be nothing else to do." He leans against it and then tries pushing hard with his head, but nothing happens. "It's too heavy for us," says Rupert. "Let's go down and tell the gentleman what we've found so far." But Edward is obstinate when he gets an idea in his mind and he insists on staying to get his breath back. "I'll have another shot soon," he puffs. Finding that his pal will not accompany him down, Rupert returns to him. "We've only pushed this great stone from one side," says Edward. "I'm not giving up until I've tried the other way." Putting his feet against the boulderhe wedges his back against another and shoves hard. "Look, it's moving!" Rupert shouts. "This isthe second time your strength has done the trick." And they gaze spellbound at what the stone has revealed.

Excitedly the two chums toil,
And scrape away the mossy soil.

Cries Edward, "Now, it's big enough,
I mean to find that silver stuff!"

The little bear is horrified
To find a deep, dark pit inside.

"I must get help without delay,
Or Edward will be there to stay!"

After the boulder has moved slightly, Edward has no difficulty in pushing it still further and Rupert cries out in excitement. "There is a space going right under the highest rock! This must prove that the message on the stick is right." Feverishly they scrape away the soil to enlarge the gap until they open up quite a big hole. It is too dark to see inside it, but Edward is now so worked up that, before Rupert can stop him, he has squeezed inside head first hoping to find the hidden treasure. Rupert watches his pal's feet anxiously. "Are you stuck? Can't you get back? Shall I pull you out?" he asks. Next minute there is a wriggle and Edward disappears, feet and all! "Hi, where have you gone?" Rupert calls, as he cautiously looks inside the space. To his horror, the hole is an entrance to a deep pit in the rock, rough and very dark. Edward's voice, rather shaky, sounds a long way down. "I must get help!" Rupert gasps as he hurries back towards the boat.

The man exclaims, "Well – any luck?"
"Yes!" Rupert calls. "But Edward's stuck!"

"Hush!" breathes the man. "What was that sound?"
"Edward!" gasps Rupert, whirling round.

The little bear calls through the crack,
"Don't worry! We'll soon have you back!"

"Quick, take this rope! Secure one end,
And drop the other to your friend."

The gentleman sees Rupert scrambling back. "Well, did you find anything up there? Is there a 'highest rock'? And . . . " "Yes," interrupts Rupert. "We found what must be the hiding place for your treasure. At least, Edward did. It's a terribly deep hole and he slithered into it and can't get out!" As he speaks there is another noise and they both turn towards the crack in the cliff. "That's Edward's voice," cries Rupert, hurrying to the gap. The gap in the cliff narrows still more, and at the end there is only a narrow crevice. "Is that you, Edward?" Rupert calls. "Are you all right?" "Yes, it's me, and I'm not hurt. I'm too tough." Edward's voice merely sounds annoyed. "I bumped my way down and couldn't stop until I landed on a sort of iron box. There's no way out except at the top!" The gentleman hears his words and calls Rupert back. "Quick, take this rope from the boat," he says. "Go up and drop one end to him!"

RUPERT HELPS WITH A ROPE

So Rupert does as he is told,
"Here comes a rope!" he cries. "Catch hold!"

"I found the treasure chest all right,"
Puffs Edward, as he comes in sight.

"Oh my, you gave us such a turn!"
The man exclaims, in great concern.

They leave the island far behind,
While Edward tells about his find.

Climbing breathlessly up the steep flank of the island Rupert reaches the highest rock and, tying one end of the rope firmly to the boulder, he drops the other end into the dark hole, calling to Edward to look out for it. Then there is an anxious wait while Rupert hears his pal grunting and puffing, but at last Edward reappears through the space under the rock. "Whew, it's good to be back in daylight!" he wheezes. "Without that rope I don't think I should ever have got out again." The gentleman is waiting near the shore, and his relief is great when he sees both the little friends coming to him. "You really ought to come up and see that hole in the rock," calls Edward, who has quickly recovered his form. "If you were there Rupert and I could both go down." "Yes, we've left the rope in position!" says Rupert. But the gentleman only grins as he hustles them into the boat and rows away. "You've had enough for today," he declares.

RUPERT IS TAKEN HOME

"Come on, you must go home and rest,
My nephews will bring up the chest."

"I hope that you enjoyed your drive,"
Smiles Mummy, when the three arrive.

No more is heard, the days go past,
And then a letter comes at last.

Cries Rupert, "Hullo, there you are!
Can you come out in Daddy's car?"

The gentleman is in great spirits as he hurries the little pals back to his car. "That box you said was at the bottom of the deep hole must be the family silver that has been lost for so long," he says. "My nephew will now recover it properly, though most of the credit goes to you two remarkable young explorers!" And in Nutwood he hands Rupert and Edward over to Mrs Bear. "I still haven't finished with these bright sparks, ma'am," he smiles. "You'll be hearing from me

again in a week or two, I hope." Many days go by and nothing happens. Then early one morning, as Rupert is helping to clean the old car, Mrs Bear hurries out. "There's a letter from that gentleman with the carved stick," she says urgently. "He wants us to meet him this very morning at Nutchester Museum and he wants us to take Edward." "Hooray, I'll find him," cries Rupert, and scampering towards Edward's cottage he spies his pal returning from the village shops.

RUPERT VISITS A MUSEUM

"That gentleman," he tells his chum,
"Would like to meet us. Do please come!"

To Nutchester Museum they ride,
Their friend is waiting just outside.

"Please come this way, and you shall see
The treasure that you found for me."

"How wonderful!" gasps Rupert Bear,
"And look! Our names are printed there!"

Rupert explains why he has come, and soon his pal is as excited as he is. "Now we shall hear whether there really was anything in that dark hole on the island," says Edward, on the way to Rupert's cottage. "It's lucky this happened today," says Mrs Bear. "It's the very last day that I've hired this funny little car." They all pile in and rattle their way into Nutchester, and there, on the steps of the Museum, they see their friend, the gentleman from the ruined castle. Inside the great building the two pals are astonished to find that there are a lot of people waiting to make a fuss of them. In a tall show-case there is a mass of glittering, silver objects of all shapes. "There you are," the gentleman smiles. "All my family treasures regained, thanks to you two. Doesn't it look lovely now!" The two friends gaze in delight, and then Rupert gives a start. For on a large card in the showcase are the words "DISCOVERED BY RUPERT BEAR AND EDWARD TRUNK."

Rupert's Decoration

Anyone can make this decoration. It's so simple that you could easily make enough to decorate a Christmas tree. Try it out with a sheet of paper about eight inches square.

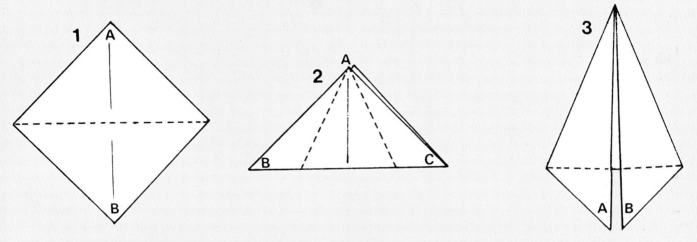

Fold the square to make a centre line AB (1), then take B up to A to give you (2). Fold edges AB and AC along the dotted lines to the centre, giving you (3). Now fold back the points A and B along the dotted lines. You have (4).

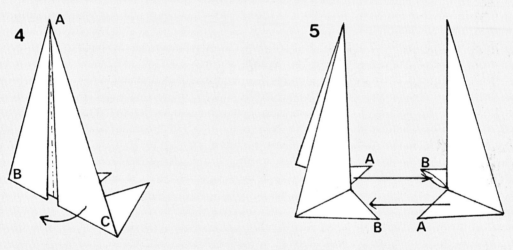

Bend the edges AB and AC towards each other so that the model looks like those in (5). Slot the points A into the pockets B to lock the two parts together.

Finally, fix a hanging thread through the points. If you can make the two parts of different coloured papers so much the better – or you could paint them. You might also try making the decorations in different sizes.

RUPERT

"What's Billy got there?" Rupert thinks.
"A box, and when it shakes it clinks."

Just a few days before Christmas Rupert is crossing Nutwood Common when he spies Billy Goat, Bill Badger and Algy Pug. Billy is holding a box and when Rupert gets near he sees that it is a money-box. "We thought it time we bought a present for Santa Claus and we're collecting for it," Billy explains. Rupert thinks this is a wonderful idea, and when he hears that his chums' parents have all given something he

and Santa Paws

*"We're sure most folk will give because
It's for a gift to Santa Claus."*

*As homeward Rupert takes the box
Across his path a small cat stalks.*

decides to take the box home to his mummy and daddy. On the way he meets a small cat he knows. "Where are you off to, Dinkie?" he asks. "I'm finding out what all my cat friends want Santa Paws to bring them at Christmas," Dinkie replies. "You mean Santa Claus," Rupert laughs. "No I don't," says the cat. "Santa Paws is a cat at Santa Claus's castle and he sends us our presents." "How odd," Rupert says and carries on home.

*"I'm calling on my cat friends 'cause
It's time we wrote to Santa Paws."*

RUPERT BUYS A PRESENT

Says Rupert, "I'll sit down and write
To Santa's Clerk this very night."

"Let's find a comfortable spot
Where we can count how much we've got."

They open up their box to count
And find they have a good amount.

"For Santa Claus this gift's just right
To keep him warm and snug at night."

Rupert is so busy that evening he thinks no more about what Dinkie has told him. Both of his parents have put money in the collecting-box and now he is writing to the Head C'`k at Santa's castle to ask if the present can be collected and kept at the castle as a surprise for Santa on Christmas morning. First thing next morning he posts the letter then goes to meet his chums with the money-box. He meets Bill and Algy near Billy Goat's cottage. "Billy's waiting for us in his garden shed to count how much money we've got," Algy says. "I say, we should be able to buy something pretty good with that," breathes Rupert when the money is spread out on the floor of the shed. And later that morning Mr Chimp the shopkeeper suggests just the thing for an old gentleman with a very cold job. "A lovely hot-water bottle to keep him warm and snug at night," he says. The chums look at each other. They nod. "Thank you, we'll take it," Rupert says.

RUPERT IS ASKED TO HELP

"Please, Rupert, when your note's written
Make out our list," asks the kitten.

He does his note to Santa Claus,
Then writes the cats' to Santa Paws.

As Dinkie leaves him Rupert spies
A tiny airplane in the skies.

"I'm sure that plane is Santa's one
To fetch the present. I must run."

Later, while Rupert is writing a note to go with Santa's present, Dinkie scratches at the window. "I've just finished a note to Santa," Rupert says as he lets the little cat in. "Yes, I thought you might be when I heard that you and your chums were sending a present to Santa," the cat says. "So I thought you'd be kind enough to write out our list for Santa Paws and send it with yours." "Oh, very well," laughs Rupert and he is soon jotting down the list of presents Dinkie dictates to him.

"Don't forget," says Dinkie as she leaves, "it's for Santa Paws not Santa Claus." At that moment Rupert hears a buzzing in the sky, and there, swooping on the village, is a tiny airplane. "I know, that must be from Santa's castle!" he exclaims and, taking the parcel and list, hurries outside. Sure enough, the little machine has landed on a flat stretch near his cottage and a small figure has climbed out and is plainly waiting for someone.

RUPERT MEETS THE CLOWN

And from the pilot's seat climbs down
A smiling figure – Santa's Clown.

"See Santa gets this, please make sure,
On Christmas Day and not before."

"Our Nutwood cats have asked if you
Will take their list of presents too."

When Santa Paws's name is used
The little Clown looks quite confused.

As Rupert hurries towards the little airplane he sees that the pilot is someone he has met before – Santa's Clown. "Hello," says the Clown briskly. "Our Head Clerk has sent me to pick up the present for Santa." Rupert hands over the parcel containing the hot-water bottle, saying, "It's important that Santa doesn't know about it until Christmas morning." "Rely on us," grins the Clown. "He'll get it at breakfast on the right morning and not a moment before."

"Oh, by the way, will you take this, too?" asks Rupert and holds out Dinkie's list. "It's a list of presents the Nutwood cats want to send to Santa Paws." The Clown hesitates. "You know, the cat at Santa's castle who looks after these things," Rupert adds. "Dinkie told me about him." Now the Clown looks quite flustered. "Oh, dear . . . I mean, oh, yes . . . um, Santa Paws," he stammers. The poor Clown is so confused that Rupert begins to wonder what can possibly have upset him so much.

RUPERT TAKES A FLIGHT

The Clown who seems quite ill at ease,
Says, "You had best come with me, please."

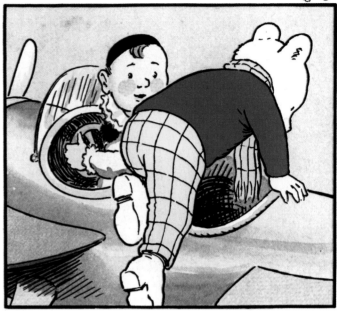

The Clown's request can't be ignored.
Though puzzled, Rupert climbs aboard.

When Rupert's safely buckled in
The Clown starts up and off they spin.

Then after an exciting flight
A towering castle comes in sight.

The Clown goes on "um-ing" and "ah-ing" for so long that Rupert has to ask, "Is something wrong?" The Clown seems to make up his mind. "Look, little bear," he says. "I think it would be best if you delivered that Santa Paws note yourself. I'll take you in the plane. There'sroom in the back." "Well, if you really think it will help," Rupert replies. "It would save a lot of bother," the Clown says. So Rupert climbs into the little airplane. "I mustn't be away for long,"

he says. "Right," says the Clown and starts the engine.In a moment the airplane is skimming along the ground and lifting into the air. Nutwood is soon left behind and on and on buzzes the little machine, most of the time through great rolling banks of clouds. At last the clouds part and ahead of them Rupert can see turrets and battlements and spires. "Santa Claus's castle," he breaths. "We've been awfully quick getting here."

RUPERT POSES A PROBLEM

As soon as they have landed there
The Clown cries, "Follow me, young bear."

"So you're the little bear who wrote
To me that very pleasant note."

"On this list are the presents that
Are wanted by each Nutwood cat."

"Oh, dear," the Clerk says, "Santa Paws!"
Then adds, "I must phone Santa Claus."

The Clown flies right among the towers and spires to land his machine on a wide terrace. He and Rupert climb down and he leads the way to an entrance guarded by toy soldiers. "It would be best if you spoke to the Head Clerk," he says. "You can give him Santa's present and the, um, list for Santa Paws." The Head Clerk, who is a bustling little man, is delighted to see Rupert. "What a pleasant letter you wrote," he smiles. "And what a lovely idea of you and your chums to give Santa a present." He takes the parcel and at the same moment spots the list Rupert has in his hand. "Is that a note to go with it?" he asks. "No, it's a present list from the Nutwood cats," Rupert replies. "It's for Santa Paws. May I take it to him? I promised he'd get it." "Santa Paws!" repeats the Head Clerk. His smile has vanished. "Oh, dear, oh, dear!" he mutters. Then he turns and picks up a telephone. "Get me Santa Claus at once," he snaps and sounds quite upset.

RUPERT WONDERS WHAT'S WRONG

*"I've talked to Santa Claus and he
Has left the whole affair to me."*

*The Clerk goes off in quite a state.
Rupert is left alone to wait.*

*He overhears while waiting there
Two workmen mention "little bear".*

*Poor Rupert thinks, "What have I done?
It seems I've upset everyone."*

"What is it about the mention of Santa Paws that seems to upset people?" Rupert wonders to himself. "Ah, Santa Claus, sir," he hears the Head Clerk say. But that is all he can make out, for the rest of the conversation is carried on in very low tones. At last the Head Clerk puts the telephone down. He doesn't look very happy. "Santa has put the matter in my hands," he says. "I shall have to leave you for a bit while I arrange things." And off he stalks, taking the Clown with him. So Rupert waits and waits. And waits some more. Two workmen pass the open door of the room where Rupert is sitting. They seem to be carrying something. They are also grumbling. "Nutwood," he hears one say, and then something about "little bear". When they pass again a little later they have another bundle and they are still complaining. "What on earth is going on?" Rupert wonders. "For some reason I seem to have upset everyone around here."

RUPERT MEETS "SANTA PAWS"

The Clown returns all puffed and blown,
Pants, "Sorry you've been left alone."

"No need to worry, little bear.
Your Santa Paws is just in there."

Then Rupert finds, before a screen,
The biggest cat he's ever seen.

"Our Nutwood cats have asked me to
Present their Christmas list to you."

A rather worried Rupert is still wondering what's wrong when the Clown hurries back, quite out of breath. "Sorry about the wait," he puffs. "Had quite a lot to do, you know." "Look," says Rupert, "what's going on? I've been left here on my own, everyone seems upset . . . " "It's all right now," interrupts the Clown. "You can come and see Santa Paws now . . . just along here." And he leads Rupert along a corridor to a plain door. "In there," he says. "Santa Paws is waiting."

The room Rupert finds himself in is rather bare. The door shuts behind him as the Clown slips away. He looks, and there on a stool sits a very large, very still, very plump cat. Timidly Rupert advances. "Ahem," he begins. "My name's Rupert and I've brought from Nutwood a list of all the presents our local cats would like at Christmas. They asked me to send it to you but the Clown said I should bring it myself . . . " Rupert stops and waits for the big fat cat to answer.

RUPERT GETS A SURPRISE

"Ah, yes, the list," the big cat squeaks.
But its mouth stays shut when it speaks.

"Do read the list," the cat says, "please."
Then comes the most almighty sneeze!

Down falls the screen. Oh, what a lark!
For there stands Santa Claus's Clerk.

"Dear me," the Clerk groans. "Lack-a-day!
Oh, what is Santa going to say?"

But at first the cat does not answer. It just stares straight ahead. So Rupert goes closer and starts to repeat what he has said. Then the cat speaks – but in a strange squeaky uncatty sort of voice. "Ah, yes, the Nutwood list. Pray read it to me," it says. "I didn't see its mouth move at all," thinks Rupert. But he doesn't remark on this and starts to read out the list of presents. Suddenly . . . Atchooo! An enormous sneeze comes from behind the screen.

Down topples the screen. And there stands the Head Clerk clutching a handkerchief to his nose. "Oh, woe is me! I've made a mess of it!" he moans through his hanky. "I-I didn't know you were there," stammers Rupert. "You weren't meant to," the Head Clerk wails. "Now the secret's out. What will Santa Claus say?" Astonishingly, all this time the cat has not stirred. It has just sat in silence, staring straight ahead with a fixed, rather silly smile.

"I had to hide in there because
There isn't any Santa Paws!"

"I fear I've bungled, little bear,
This silly Santa Paws affair."

"Here's Santa's room," the Clerk says. "Do
Let him explain it all to you."

"Well, Rupert Bear," laughs Santa Claus.
"So you've been seeing Santa Paws!"

The Head Clerk lifts down the cat and wearily sinks onto its place on the stool. He pats the cat. "Just a toy," he says. "With me trying to sound like its voice . . . you see, little bear, there is no Santa Paws . . . " "But Dinkie was so sure that there was," interrupts Rupert. "That's just the trouble," says the Head Clerk. "When you asked to see Santa Paws I was given the job of thinking of something . . . alas! Now, Santa will have to explain things to you after all. Follow me." And the little man leads Rupert up some steps to a door marked "Private". He knocks and then ushers Rupert into the room where Santa Claus himself is standing. "Put in a good word for me," the Head Clerk whispers as he slips away. Santa Claus looks at Rupert then breaks into a big smile. "So you've been seeing Santa Paws," he says. "Tell me all about it. But let's make ourselves a bit more comfortable." And plonking himself down in a fireside chair he lifts Rupert onto his knee.

*"All little kittens believe that
There is a Father Christmas cat."*

*"Since 'Santa Paws' is really me,
Their presents list I'd better see."*

*Now Rupert gladly gives his word
That he'll keep secret what he's heard.*

*The little Clerk says, "Tell me, pray,
Oh, what did Santa have to say?"*

When Rupert has finished telling Santa Claus all about Dinkie and the Nutwood cats and their note to Santa Paws and the rest, Santa Claus says, "Oh, well, now you know there is not a Santa Paws, so I'd better explain. You see, all mother cats tell their kittens about Santa Paws and how he brings their presents. Of course, I really do it but we like them to think there's a Santa Paws. But then you asked to see him and we had to do something quickly. Now let me have their list and I'll see they get their presents." He studies the list. "No trouble there," he says. "Now you'd best be getting home, young Rupert." Then as Rupert thanks him for telling him about Santa Paws, the old gentleman adds, "Ah, now, that must remain a secret. Tell your parents if you like, but only them . . . oh, and tell my Head Clerk not to worry." As Rupert emerges, the Head Clerk is waiting anxiously. "It's all right," Rupert whispers. "He's not cross with you."

RUPERT FLIES HOME

"He wasn't cross. You needn't fret.
Oh, look! The little Clown's all set."

"Your gift to Santa Claus will stay
A secret until Christmas day."

Tucked snugly in the little plane,
Rupert is flown back home again.

"Of course," says Mrs Bear, "we'll keep
Your secret. Now, then, off to sleep."

The little Head Clerk cheers up and says, "You do see, don't you, my little pretence was just so that all the kittens shouldn't be upset by learning there wasn't a special Santa for them?" "Of course," says Rupert as they walk towards the Clown's waiting airplane. "And I've promised to keep the secret." When he is safely settled in the airplane the Head Clerk says to him, "We'll keep your secret too. Santa won't know a thing about your present until Christmas morning."

Although the flight to Nutwood is just as fast as the trip to Santa's castle it is dusk by the time the airplane touches down near Rupert's cottage. Rupert bids the Clown a hasty goodbye and dashes indoors where Mrs Bear is beginning to wonder where he's got to. He has so much to tell her that he is still talking as he sips his bedtime drink. "And you won't tell anyone at all about Santa Paws?" he ends up. "Daddy and I won't say a word about it," promises Mrs Bear.

Though Rupert tells of where he's been,
He doesn't mention cat or screen.

Says Mr Bear, "I hope that you
Will bring your pals at Christmas too."

"Oh, Merry Christmas!" Rupert cries,
And to his pile of presents flies.

That morning Dinkie comes to show
Her beautiful new silky bow.

Next day Rupert meets Algy and tells him all about his adventure. Well, not quite all. For, of course, he has promised not to breathe a word to anyone else about Santa Paws. "The Head Clerk at Santa's Castle has promised that Santa will get our present at breakfast on Christmas Day," he says. Just then the chums are joined by Mr Bear carrying a fine Christmas tree he has been buying. "Hello, young Algy," he says. "I hope we'll see you on Christmas morning, and do bring the other chums." "We'll be there," the little pug laughs.

On Christmas morning Rupert is up very early. "Merry Christmas, Mummy and Daddy!" he cries as he rushes into the room. "And, oooh! All my presents have come!" As he unwraps them he has a thought: "Of course, Santa will be opening our present to him. Hope he likes it." Breakfast is just over when there is a mewing outside. And there at the door is Dinkie in a new silk bow.

RUPERT IS THANKED

*"All Nutwood's cats have asked me to
Pass on their kindest thanks to you."*

*"Please, Rupert," Dinkie asks, "do write
Our thanks to Santa Paws tonight."*

*As Dinkie stalks off Bill guffaws,
"That's silly! She said Paws not Claus!"*

*"That's Santa's message and it's meant
To say he likes the gift we sent."*

"This is the bow I asked Santa Paws for," the little cat says. "I've come round to tell you that all my friends have got what they wanted and to give you our thanks." Just then there are cries of "Merry Christmas, Rupert!" and Billy Goat, Algy and Bill appear. "Since you seem to have visitors I shan't keep you," Dinkie says. "But just one thing more. Because you're so good at writing things will you be kind enough to send our thanks to Santa Paws?"

As Dinkie struts away Bill chuckles, "I say, did you hear that? Dinkie said Santa Paws instead of Santa Claus." Luckily Rupert doesn't have to reply for just then Algy exclaims, "Look! That plane is writing in smoke . . . 'Santa's thanks'." "That's the Clown's airplane," Rupert cries. "I flew in it to Santa's castle. Santa Claus really must have sent it to let us know he really likes our hot-water bottle present. Now we can all really enjoy Christmas day!"

Freddy the Fox

Use a 5" to 7" square of paper, white on one side, black (or brown) on the other. Always check your fold in the next diagram.

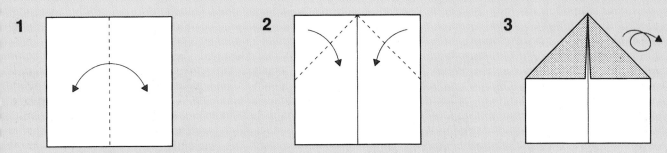

(1) White side up. Fold in half. Unfold. (2) Fold corners to centre line. (3) Turn model over - like turning a page in a book.

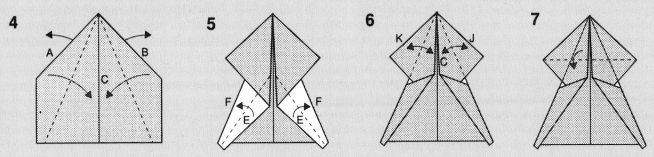

(4) Fold so edge 'A' lies along centre line 'C', let the flap underneath come out. Now do the same with 'B'. (5) Fold edge 'E' along 'F' (both sides) (6) Fold edge 'J' along centre line 'C' and *open up* do the same with 'K' (7) Fold along dashed line.

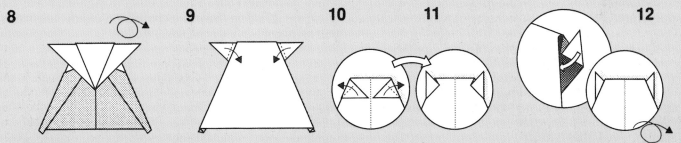

(8) Turn over like a page in a book. (9) Fold little flaps (ears) or dashed line. (10) Now fold the corners out again on dashed line. (11) This is the result now lift each ear tucked *under* the top layer. (12) This is the ear being tucked under - do both now turn over.

(13) Fold up and crease on dashed line (about 1/3 of the way to the nose of the fox). (14) Hold each leg *below* the fold you made in step 13. Twist a little so your thumbs are on top and fingers below, now move the hands away from each other so the paper is tight - then bring the hands closer and Freddy will nod. (15) Move fingers together and then pull first one leg and then the other downwards; Freddy will put his head on one side.

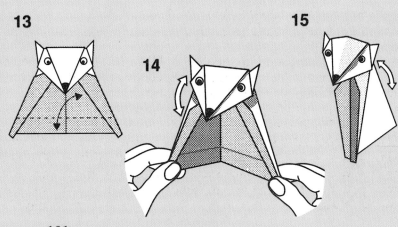

RUPERT and

One morning, after Christmas Day,
Rupert decides to go and play . . .

Christmas Day has been and gone in Nutwood and Rupert and his parents have enjoyed a wonderful break . . . "I think I'll go up to the common to see if I can find any chums to play with," says Rupert. "Good idea," smiles Mrs Bear "You can invite them back for some mince pies if you like!" To Rupert's delight, several of his pals have had the same idea. Before long, they are all happily playing football together, each taking a turn in goal . . .

he Christmas Box

The chums play football – everyone
Joins in and all enjoy the fun.

"I'll see you later!" Rupert cries.
"Come round and have some hot mince pies!"

When the game ends, Rupert invites his pals to drop by later. "Thanks!" says Bill. "That would be great. You can show me your presents. I'd better go and let my parents know first. Perhaps you can come and visit us tomorrow . . . " When Rupert gets home, he is surprised to see an unopened parcel standing all alone, under the Christmas tree. "That's odd!" he blinks. "I'm sure we opened everything on Christmas Day. I don't remember any gifts being left behind . . . "

He arrives home, surprised to find
A present that's been left behind . . .

RUPERT HAS AN EXTRA PRESENT

"A box!" says Rupert. "Somebody
Has sent it to us specially."

"How odd!" blinks Mrs Bear. "I'm sure
I didn't see it there before . . . "

"Who can it be from? We'll soon know –
As soon as I untie the bow . . . "

As Rupert watches, Mr Bear
Exclaims, "Bless me! There's nothing there!"

Picking up the mystery gift, Rupert finds that it is a brightly painted box, with a ribbon tied round it . . . "Perhaps somebody delivered it while I was out?" he thinks. "I wonder if Mum and Dad know what's inside?" When Rupert shows the box to his parents, they are just as surprised to see it as he was . . . "How very strange!" says Mrs Bear. "We haven't had any callers all morning." "The Postman hasn't been either!" blinks Rupert's father. "I wonder who it's from?"

"I suppose we must have just missed this on Christmas Day!" says Rupert's father as he unties the ribbon round the mysterious box. "If it was mixed up with all the others, it might have got pushed behind the tree . . . " "Perhaps," says Mrs Bear. "But I'm sure I haven't seen it before!" Rupert looks on expectantly as his father releases a catch and opens the box's hinged lid. "Bless me!" he blinks. "This is stranger than ever! It's completely empty. There's nothing inside at all . . . "

RUPERT'S PAL OPENS THE BOX

*"It's very strange! Perhaps someone
Just thought they'd play a joke, for fun . . . "*

*"Hello, Bill! Come inside and see
What we found, underneath our tree."*

*"Whoever sent it left no name –
Guess what's inside! Let's play a game . . . "*

*"A toy!" laughs Bill as Rupert cries
"Impossible!" and rubs his eyes.*

Rupert and his parents are completely mystified by the empty box . . . "What a strange thing to send anyone for Christmas!" he thinks. "I wonder if there's meant to be anything inside, or if someone's just playing a joke?" He is still looking at the box when Bill arrives. "You didn't send me a wooden box tied up with ribbon, did you?" asks Rupert. "Me?" blinks Bill. "No, why?" "Come and see!" says Rupert. "We've had a strange delivery and nobody knows who it's from . . . "

Without saying another word, Rupert leads his chum in to see the strange box . . . "What do you make of it?" he asks. "Looks like a Jack-in-the-Box to me," says Bill. "Don't say you haven't opened it yet? How could you resist?" "Have a look inside," urges Rupert. "Go on, tell me what you see . . . " Releasing the catch, Bill opens the lid and smiles. "Very nice!" he laughs. "But why all the mystery?" "It . . . it is a Jack-in-the-Box!" blinks Rupert. "But that's impossible!"

"The box was empty, Bill, I swear!
We looked inside – nothing was there . . . "

Before Rupert says any more,
Another chum knocks at the door.

"Hello Podgy! Let's see if you
Can guess what's inside this box too . . . "

"Toffees!" smiles Podgy. "What a treat!
I do like presents you can eat!"

"What's so strange about a Jack-in-the-Box?" asks Bill. "Nothing," blinks Rupert. "It's just that it wasn't there last time I looked! When the box arrived it was completely empty . . . " "Perhaps it has a secret compartment?" suggests Bill. "Close the lid and see what happens if you open it again . . . " The chums are just about to release the catch when Mrs Bear appears with another Christmas visitor. "Hello!" says Podgy. "I came as soon as I could. I hope I'm not too late for the mince pies . . . "

"Never mind mince pies!" says Rupert. "What do you think is inside this box, Podgy? It's a mystery present that suddenly appeared under our tree . . . " "It looks like a box of sweets to me!" smiles Podgy. "Toffees!" he laughs as Rupert releases the catch. "They're my favourites! It's full to the brim. What a marvellous Christmas treat! I expect it's from one of your uncles. Uncle Bruno often sends presents. Perhaps it's from him? The label's probably fallen off in the post . . . "

RUPERT MAKES A WISH

"Toffees!" blinks Bill. "It can't be true!
Now I'm as mystified as you . . . "

"It must be magic!" Rupert beams.
"The box gives what you want, it seems . . . "

"I'll ask for something now. I know!
I wish that we could have some snow . . . "

As Rupert peers in, he can feel
Cold snowflakes on his face . . . "They're real!"

"Toffees!" gasps Bill. "Where have they come from? I don't understand . . . " "Neither do I!" blinks Mrs Bear. "I thought the box was empty!" "It was," says Rupert. "The first time we looked there was nothing there. Then there was a Jack-in-the-Box, now it's full of sweets! I wonder? Let's close the lid and see what happens next." "What do you think's going on?" asks Bill. "Magic!" smiles Rupert. "I think the box grants wishes. Everyone who opens it gets something different . . . "

"A wishing-box!" blinks Bill. "What are you going to ask it for?" "I don't know," says Rupert. "The only thing I'd really like is some snow to go sledging. I don't suppose the box can grant wishes like that . . . " Releasing the catch, he slowly opens the lid then peers inside. To Rupert's astonishment, a cold wind blows into his face, followed by flakes of snow which swirl into the room in a miniature blizzard . . . "I don't believe it!" cries Bill. "It's exactly what you asked for!"

RUPERT TAKES THE BOX OUTSIDE

"Quick, Rupert! Take that box of yours
And put it somewhere safe, outdoors . . . "

"What's that?" blinks Mr Bear. "Oh, dear!
How did a snowstorm get in here?"

The three chums run outside. "Now where?
The common! We can leave it there . . . "

The box keeps sending out more snow
Until a blizzard starts to blow!

"It's snowing indoors!" cries Mrs Bear. "Rupert! Do something! Take that thing outside . . . " Seizing the box, Rupert runs from the room, while Bill hurries ahead of him to open the front door. The pair dash past an astonished Mr Bear, who clearly can't believe his eyes. "It's snow!" cries Podgy. "Real snow! I'd rather have more toffees myself but you have to admit it's spectacular!" "Snow?" gasps Rupert's father. "But what's it doing in here? It's not even snowing outside . . . "

Clutching the wishing-box tightly, Rupert runs away from his house and up on to Nutwood Common. "What now?" calls Bill as he and Podgy follow closely behind. "We'll leave it up here!" decides Rupert. "The snow won't bother anyone and we might even get a patch to play on." "Good idea!" laughs Podgy. "It's still swirling up like a blizzard. I wonder if it will go on for long?" "Who knows?" shrugs Rupert. "The box seems to work by magic. I suppose it will just keep snowing until we've had enough . . . "

RUPERT SEES THICK SNOW

The three friends watch delightedly –
Then hurry home in time for tea . . .

"Well done!" says Mrs Bear. "That box
Had far too many tricks and shocks!"

Next morning, Rupert wakes to find
The box has left his wish behind . . .

"The whole of Nutwood's covered in
Thick snow!" calls Rupert with a grin.

As the pals stand watching the box, it sends out more and more snow, till a great cloud hangs over Nutwood Common. "Fantastic!" cheers Bill. "If it settles we can go sledging after all!" "Tomorrow will tell!" says Podgy. "We'd better go home now, before it gets dark!" "See you tomorrow," calls Rupert. "I'll keep my fingers crossed!" When he gets home, Mrs Bear has almost finished clearing up after the unexpected snowstorm. "Well done!" she tells Rupert. "We can't have blizzards in the house!" The next morning, Mrs Bear comes in to wake Rupert early with some surprising news . . . "Just wait until you look outside!" she says. "It looks as thought that box of yours has covered the whole of Nutwood!" Jumping out of bed, Rupert hurries over to the window and gazes out on a thick, crisp coat of snow. "Wonderful!" he laughs. "It's just what I wanted. Now the box has granted my wish too. I'll be able to go out with the others and play in the snow all day!"

RUPERT PLAYS WITH HIS CHUMS

*"Look out!" laughs Bill as Rupert comes
Across the snow to join his chums . . .*

*The pals throw snowballs. Everyone
Joins in and shares the winter fun.*

*"The box!" says Bill. "Let's go and see
What the next wish it grants will be . . . "*

*"Look, there!" blinks Rupert. "This is weird!
The magic box has disappeared!"*

When Rupert reaches the common he finds his chums have all come to play in the snow . . . "Isn't this wonderful?" calls Bill. "It's just what we need!" The pals are soon having a snowball fight with Podgy and Willie taking on the others. "Bull's eye!" laughs Podgy as he catches Algy. "My turn now!" calls Rupert. "Look out, Willie!" When they have had enough of snowballs the friends take turns on Algy's sledge, which speeds over the freshly fallen snow all the way to the bottom of the

hill . . . Rupert and his friends enjoy playing in the snow so much that they nearly forget all about the magic box . . . "I wonder if it will grant any more wishes?" says Bill. "We've all had a turn, but Willie and Algy might like to try their luck." The pals start looking for the high rock where Rupert stood the box. "Up there!" he cries. "I'm sure that's where we left it." "You're right," blinks Bill. "But there's nothing there now. The box has disappeared! I wonder where it's gone?"

RUPERT FOLLOWS A TRAIL

"Fresh footprints! Look, I've found a clue!
Someone's taken the box, but who?"

"This way!" says Rupert. "We'll soon find
The thieves. They've left a trail behind!"

"It's Farmer Brown's hut! Someone's there!
Two sets of footprints. It's a pair . . . "

"There's someone groaning!" Rupert blinks.
"They don't sound very well!" he thinks.

The chums are still puzzling over the disappearance of the magic box when Willie Mouse spots a trail of footprints in the snow . . . "Two people!" he calls. "They must have found the box and carried it off." "You might be right," nods Rupert. "I can see two sets of prints. They seem to lead along this way and over the brow of that hill . . . " "Fresh this morning!" says Podgy as the chums follow the trail. "Whoever made them must have been here early, just before we arrived . . . "

Rupert and his pals follow the trail of footprints across the common until they reach an old shed by the side of a copse. "Farmer Brown's shelter!" says Bill. "He sometimes uses it to store things. You don't suppose he's the one who's taken the box, do you?" "No," whispers Rupert. "There are two sets of footprints, side by side . . . " "Who can it be?" asks his chum as the pair tip-toe forward. "Listen!" says Rupert suddenly. "I can hear someone groaning. They don't sound very happy . . . "

"The Fox brothers! I might have known!"
But what has made them wail and groan?

"It started with a box we found
Left empty, lying on the ground . . . "

"I took the box, then heard it make
A sound each time I gave a shake . . . "

"The empty box was full somehow,
Of chocolate decorations now!"

"Freddy and Ferdy!" cries Rupert as the chums peer inside the shed. The Fox brothers are sitting near the open box, surrounded by brightly-coloured pieces of foil . . . "Er, hello, Rupert," says Freddy. "You're too late for a chocolate decoration, I'm afraid. We've just finished the last one." "I wish we hadn't!" groans Ferdy. "I never want to see another as long as I live!" "Do you know who the box belongs to?" asks his brother. "We found it out in the snow and decided to keep it . . . "

"The box was empty when we found it!" says Freddy. "I thought it might be useful for keeping things in, but then, as we were on our way home, it suddenly started to rattle . . . " "We opened the lid and found it was full of chocolate Christmas tree decorations!" adds Ferdy. "Just what we wanted, as all ours were finished by Christmas Day . . . " "They tasted delicious!" says his brother. "I still don't know where they came from, but it was just like having someone grant a wish . . . "

RUPERT TAKES THE BOX HOME

"We can't eat any more today!
You'd better take the box away . . . "

"Poor things! They got their wish but still
Just ended up by feeling ill!"

"I'll take the box back home with me
And store it somewhere properly . . . "

But Mrs Bear is horrified –
"No, Rupert! Take that box outside!"

At first, Rupert thinks the Fox brothers mean to keep the magic box, but, to his surprise, they are quite happy to give it away . . . "No more chocolates for us!" groans Freddy. "I don't even want to open the lid and see if there are any more! You keep the box, Rupert. I'm going home for a lie down . . . " "Me too!" says Ferdy. "See you later, everyone." "Poor things!" says Rupert as the pair stagger off. "They did get a wish but it looks as though they'd have been better off without it!"

Glad to have recovered the box, Rupert tells the others he'll take it home with him for safe-keeping. "Good idea!" calls Bill. "We can try making another wish tomorrow!" When Rupert carries his prize into the house, Mrs Bear is far less pleased to see it . . . "Not in here!" she cries. "I don't want any more showers of indoor snow! Put that box in the garden shed if you want to keep it. Goodness knows what it will come up with next! We'll store it outside where it can't do any harm . . . "

"Somebody sent the box, but who?"
Says Mrs Bear. "I wish we knew . . . "

The lid flies open. Smoke pours out
And coloured stars swirl all about . . .

"Look!" Rupert calls as the smoke clears –
His friend, The Sage of Um, appears.

"A spell I made went badly wrong –
I've been trapped inside all along!"

Rupert and his mother go out to the garden shed. While he unlocks the door, Mrs Bear looks thoughtfully at the box. "I wish we knew who its owner was . . . " she murmurs. As she speaks, the lid flies open with a puff of coloured smoke. Stars swirl all around the astonished pair. "More tricks!" wails Rupert's mother. "I might have known something like this would happen!" To Rupert's amazement, the clearing smoke reveals a shadowy figure – who seems almost as surprised as the startled onlookers . . . "The Sage of Um!" cries Rupert as he recognises the unexpected visitor. "Oh, dear!" blinks Mrs Bear. "His foot's stuck in the box . . ." "Don't worry!" smiles the Sage. "There's no need for alarm. I have been stuck for a week or so, but your final wish has just set me free . . ." "Stuck inside the box?" asks Rupert as he helps his old friend up. "Exactly!" says the Sage. "A spell that went wrong, I'm afraid. The box was only meant to contain your Christmas presents . . . "

RUPERT GETS SOME SKIS

"I muddled up the Sending Spell
And sent myself along as well!"

"I know it's late, but in here too
Are presents that I've brought for you . . . "

"I wonder what it is I've got?
There's something here. I can't see what . . . "

The box has one last big surprise –
"A pair of skis! Look!" Rupert cries.

"I thought it would be fun to fill a box with presents for Nutwood," explains the Sage. "It was meant to arrive on Christmas Day. Everything was fine until I tried out the Sending Spell . . . I'm afraid I got the last verse muddled and sent myself as well!" "Goodness!" blinks Rupert's mother. "So you spent the whole holiday trapped inside . . . " "Indeed!" nods the Sage. "Still, better late than never! Your presents are in here too, you know. Open the lid and help yourselves . . . "

As the Sage of Um holds the box, Rupert reaches inside and feels for a parcel. "It's just like the Lucky Dip at Nutwood's Summer Fair!" he smiles. "Catch hold and pull!" laughs his friend. To Rupert's amazement, he finds himself holding a set of skis, all tied together with a bright red ribbon. "I don't believe it!" blinks Mrs Bear. "How did they fit into the little box?" "Magic!" beams the Sage. "I hope you like them, Rupert. Just the thing for a snowy, white Christmas . . . "

RUPERT'S FRIENDS SAY GOODBYE

It's Mrs Bear's turn. "Mitts! How nice!
They're perfect for the snow and ice . . . "

The Sage declares that he must go –
"I'll leave you to enjoy the snow!"

"Farewell!" the Sage calls. Stars appear –
"I hope you have a happy year . . . "

"What fun!" laughs Rupert. "I can ski!
Hi, everybody! Look at me . . . "

"Your turn now!" the Sage tells Mrs Bear. Rupert's mother reaches deep into the box and pulls out a pair of new winter mittens . . . "Wonderful!" she laughs. "I'll wear them straightaway." "Time I was getting back to Um Island, now," says the Sage. "The unicorns will be wondering where I've got to!" "Can't you stay for tea and mince pies?" asks Mrs Bear. "Next year, perhaps," smiles the Sage. "Right now, there's no time to lose. One more spell and I'll be gone . . . "

"Goodbye, everyone!" calls the Sage as he waves his magic wand in a swirl of stars. "Have a happy new year . . . " As Rupert looks on, his friend suddenly vanishes – together with the box which has made Nutwood's Christmas so extraordinary . . . "Never mind!" smiles Mrs Bear. "At least we've still got lots of snow! You'll be able to try out your new skis." "Good idea!" says Rupert. "Wait until I tell the others where they came from. What a marvellous present . . . "

THE END

Follow
RUPERT
in the
DAILY
EXPRESS
every morning

80 *Years of* RUPERT *Annuals*

A Christmas tradition from 1936 to 2016!

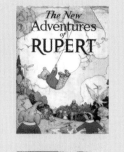